A Refuge of Lies

Studies in Violence, Mimesis, and Culture

The Studies in Violence, Mimesis, and Culture Series examines issues related to the nexus of violence and religion in the genesis and maintenance of culture. It furthers the agenda of the Colloquium on Violence and Religion, an international association that draws inspiration from René Girard's mimetic hypothesis on the relationship between violence and religion, elaborated in a stunning series of books he has written over the last forty years. Readers interested in this area of research can also look to the association's journal, *Contagion: Journal of Violence, Mimesis, and Culture.*

A Refuge of Lies

REFLECTIONS ON FAITH AND FICTION

Cesáreo Bandera

Michigan State University Press · *East Lansing*

♾ The paper used in this publication meets the minimum requirements of ANSI/NISO Z39.48-1992 (R 1997) (Permanence of Paper).

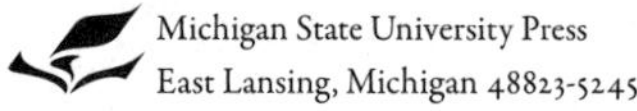
Michigan State University Press
East Lansing, Michigan 48823-5245

Printed and bound in the United States of America.

19 18 17 16 15 14 13 1 2 3 4 5 6 7 8 9 10

LIBRARY OF CONGRESS CATALOGING-IN-PUBLICATION DATA
Bandera, Cesareo.
A refuge of lies : reflections on faith and fiction / Cesareo Bandera.
pages cm. — (Studies in violence, mimesis, and culture series)
Includes bibliographical references.
ISBN 978-1-60917-378-4 (ebook) — ISBN 978-1-61186-088-7 (pbk. : alk. paper)
1. Religion and literature. 2. Philosophy and religion in literature. 3. Mimesis. 4. Truth in literature. I. Title.
PN49.B1367 2013
809'.93382—dc23
2012049421

Book design by Charlie Sharp, Sharp Des!gns, Lansing, Michigan
Cover design by David Drummond, Salamander Design, www.salamanderhill.com
Cover image is *The Procession of the Trojan Horse into Troy,* circa 1760, by Giandomenico Tiepolo (1727–1804). Oil on canvas, 38.8 × 66.7 cm. (NG3319), © National Gallery, London/Art Resource, NY.

green press INITIATIVE Michigan State University Press is a member of the Green Press Initiative and is committed to developing and encouraging ecologically responsible publishing practices. For more information about the Green Press Initiative and the use of recycled paper in book publishing, please visit *www.greenpressinitiative.org.*

Visit Michigan State University Press at *www.msupress.org*

Contents

To Gabriel, budding young writer

Prologue

> And when he was alone, those who were about him with the twelve asked him concerning the parables. And he said to them, "To you has been given the mystery of the kingdom of God, but for those outside everything is in parables; so that they may indeed see but not perceive, and may indeed hear but not understand; lest they should convert, and be forgiven." And he said to them, "Do you not understand this parable? How then will you understand all the parables?"
>
> —Mark 4, 11–13

Strange words, indeed. But not the shocking thing that many people imagine. Christ speaks in universal terms. Let me paraphrase: "The word of God has been revealed to you, but for those outside this revelation everything is in parables, they have been given nothing but parables, fictions. They do not have the meaning beyond the fiction. They see, but do not really see, for they cannot get beyond the letter; they hear, but do not understand. They cannot convert, and have their sins forgiven. For conversion and forgiveness is only through the revelation. Thus he also said to them: "How is it that you do not understand this parable [of the sower]? How will you, then, understand all parables, all narrative fictions? The key has already been given to you."

This book can be viewed as an extended commentary on this gospel passage. Interpreters think the parables are there to explain the kingdom of God, but that only works on the basis of a prior view of all parables, all fiction, in the light of the mystery of the kingdom, which is what gives them ultimate meaning. In a sense, fictions must be redeemed before they can become instruments of redemption. Otherwise—the gospel says—they will block the path to conversion and forgiveness. They will become a stumbling block, a scandal. But this also means that beyond the space where the word of God is historically revealed lies an "outside," a world where everything is turned to fiction (*en parabolais ta panta ginetai*), literally. And that is Homer's world. We begin there.

Introduction

Erich Auerbach's *Mimesis: The Representation of Reality in Western Literature*, published more than sixty years ago, and reprinted more recently in 2003 with an introduction by Edward W. Said, is quite deservedly already a classic. Auerbach brought into high relief the striking and fundamental difference that exists between the two basic approaches to the textual representation of reality in Western culture. These two "styles," as he called them, were archetypically displayed in Homer's poems and in the Old Testament respectively: "Since we are using the two styles, the Homeric and the Old Testament, as starting points, we have taken them as finished products, as they appear in the texts . . . for it is in their full development, which they reached in early times, that the two styles exercised their determining influence upon the representation of reality in European literature" (23).[1] That is also the starting point of the present study, which would like to take Auerbach's basic intuition much further than he probably intended or could have anticipated.

To begin with, among the numerous stylistic differences brilliantly analyzed by the critic, a deeper difference emerges that both transcends and grounds all the others. It concerns the truth of each of the two archetypal texts, or rather, the attitude exhibited in those texts with regard to the truth of what they narrate. Coming to the Bible after an extensive and meticulous analysis of Homer's style, Auerbach is indeed quite properly amazed at the Bible's "passionate" concern for, and interest in, the truth of what it says. For that is precisely what he never found in Homer.

I share Auerbach's amazement, but I think he did not quite see the scope, the full extent, of the difference. His explanation only goes part of the way, and in that sense it is ultimately misleading. The Bible—he says—must be vitally concerned about the truth of what it narrates, because "the existence of the sacred ordinances of life [of the Jewish people] rested upon [its] truth" (14). In other words, to the biblical narrator, what he narrates is not only historically, objectively, true, it is also sacred. A proposition that must be understood both ways: what he narrates is believed to be historically true *because* it is viewed as sacred, and it is sacred *because* it is seen as the truth. What Auerbach actually saw in the Bible was an unwavering belief in the intimate connection between historical reality, the reality of the world that is *truly* out there, and the sacred.

However, as soon as we bring the very notion of the sacred into focus, we must realize that we are dealing with something rather ambiguous—in fact, radically protean, not easily pinned down. It can elicit different, even contradictory, reactions among its devotees. In the case of the biblical narrator, whether Elohist or Yahwist, the sacred truth calls clearly for adherence and trust. But does that mean that the truth which Homer consistently avoids, never concerning himself with it directly, is therefore not sacred to him? Is truth deliberately avoided necessarily less sacred than truth openly proclaimed? That seems to be Auerbach's assumption, for he shows no surprise at all in the face of Homer's apparently complete lack of interest in historical reality, in the truth of what he narrates. Auerbach takes for granted that Homer is only interested in creating his own poetic reality, which is "good enough" for him and for his original audience. In other words, religion does not explain anything fundamental in Homer's style. If it did, if he felt he was dealing with something sacred, so goes the inner logic of the argument, Homer would be more concerned with the truth of what he narrates, less absorbed in his own make-believe, poetic world.

But, in principle, this assumption is anthropologically incorrect. Sacred dealings, religious intent, do not imply allegiance to, or trust in, the truth necessarily. Quite the opposite: by and large what we find in archaic religion is an intimate association of the sacred with secrecy; with avoidance and hiding of the truth; with an immemorial, collectively inherited sense that the truth as such, beyond whatever its circumstances may be in any given situation, is something dangerous that can only be approached cautiously, and must be surrounded by strict prohibitions, taboos. We encounter this notion from very primitive societies[2] to the famous mystery cults of Greco-Roman religion, for example. Occasionally the so-called "mysteries" of these cults have been equated to the "mysteries" of Christianity. But the comparison can only illustrate the fundamental difference between the two: the only mystery of the Eleusinian, the Orphic, or any other pagan cult is the one created by the prohibition imposed on its initiates against divulging whatever ceremonies were performed in their secret meetings. The specific content of what they did in secret may have been completely trivial, but it acquired the character of sacred truth as soon as it was made secret, as soon as it was prohibited to bring it out in the open. The Christian mysteries are real, rational mysteries; they have nothing to do with fear of the truth. To put it in the perceptive words of G. K. Chesterton, "Always, it has been truly said, the savage is talkative about his mythology and taciturn about his religion."[3] It was also Chesterton who noticed these two intimately related things in pagan religion and poetry in general: a profound absence, a strange silence, behind all the tall tales of mythology, and an "unfathomable sadness" (93). These are Chesterton's words:

> I am concerned rather with an internal than an external truth; and . . . the internal truth is almost indescribable. We have to speak of something of which it is the whole point that people did not speak of it; we have not merely to translate from a strange tongue or speech, but from a strange silence. (92)

Therefore, against this general pagan background, the "passionate" concern for the truth that Auerbach correctly finds in the Bible is indeed exceptional. And it is exceptional precisely because of the sacred character of the text. On the other hand, Homer's "poetic" forgetfulness of the truth appears to be much more in keeping with the sacred rule that prevails in nonbiblical archaic traditions.

In other words, we want to examine in this study the possibility that

Homer's "poetic" disregard for the truth may be just as sacred, as obligatory, and essential to him as the "passionate" concern for the truth is to the biblical narrator. But if this is so, we will have to find an explanation for the archaic fear of the truth—or, to be more precise, archaic fear of the sacred character of the truth, fear of the truth because it is unavoidably tied to the sacred, in contrast to which stands the biblical faith in the truth. In spite of appearances, Homer's poetic "reality" may be a rather archaic sacred instrument. We moderns (even postmoderns) can understand having faith in the truth, but we do not understand fearing the truth as such: not this or that circumstantial truth, but the truth as truth, as that which reveals the world out there as being out there *truly* or *in truth*, or *in reality*—in other words, that which reveals the *reality*, the *being-there*, of that which is out there. Animals know that there is something out there, but they do not know that something is *truly* out there. To human beings, not only the thing is meaningful, but the being there of the thing as well. Truth as *aletheia* (as "unconcealment" in a Heideggerian sense)[4] is precisely what reveals and gives meaning to the being-there-ness of the world out there. And that is the work of the spirit, not the senses; that is, in other words, sacred.

In his *Questiones de veritate*, Saint Thomas Aquinas says the following:

> In a natural thing, truth is found especially in the first [i.e., conformity with the divine rather than the human intellect], rather than in the second, sense; for its reference to the divine intellect comes before its reference to a human intellect. Even if there were no human intellects, things could be said to be true because of their relation to the divine intellect. But if, by an impossible supposition, intellect did not exist and things did continue to exist, then the essentials of truth would in no way remain. (*Q.* 1, art. 2)[5]

We could put it in a modern way that takes into account scientific advances. In the words of Wolfhardt Pannenberg:

> How can we understand the fact that human consciousness and language are capable of grasping the nature of things? The possibility that human propositions can be true would present great difficulties if human consciousness were entirely passive and pure receptivity in its perceptions. But today we know that it is quite otherwise. Consciousness and the

> brain are most active when something is experienced, beginning with sense perception. How, then, is it possible that information we receive is not hopelessly falsified? On the basis of the biblical view of spirit and consciousness, we could answer that the possibility of grasping reality external to ourselves with our consciousness is founded in the fact that the Spirit in which we participate is also the origin of all life external to us, the origin of all forms of created reality. . . . Only because the Spirit grounds all created reality can it also be the origin of a consciousness that grasps things as what they are in themselves. . . . Such suggestions accommodate the findings of today's natural scientists, according to which modern physics no longer offers a materialistic description of the universe. In reference to the development of physics from classical mechanics, with its fundamental concept of the body, to the rise of the idea of field as the fundamental concept of modern physics and its attempts to derive matter itself from nonmaterial states, Karl Popper also says, "Materialism transcends itself." On the basis of similar considerations, theoretical physicist Georg Süssman writes, "Thus the material of all things appears to be as if crafted out of thought."[6]

Or in the philosophical language of phenomenology:

> Logical truth presupposes the mutual being—ordained of intellect and existent. . . . But the existent is insufficiently described if we consider it only as such or as it is in itself. *It pertains to its nature to manifest itself*, i.e., to be at least accessible to the knowing intellect, if not—as is the case with the knowledge which the divine intellect has of existents—immediately transparent. *And in relation to what "any existent" is in itself, its manifestation or revelation, or its being ordained to the spirit, are something new.*[7]

In any case, truth, which is originally the truth of the world out there, is strictly for humans, who in knowing that the world out there is truly out there, know something divine, enter into some sort of communication with God. If, as St. Thomas says, "by an impossible supposition," things could exist without God, they would lose their truth. And we may add: if, by another impossible supposition, human beings could continue to exist with things, but without God, human beings would never know those things were true.

Just like animals (or creatures without intellect) who, though they know, they do not know the truth of what they know. Thus St. Thomas again:

> Although sense knows that it senses, it does not know its own nature; consequently, it knows neither the nature of its act nor the proportion of this act to things. As a result, it does not know its truth. (1, art. 9)

But St. Thomas, or the line of thought that originated with him, can only take us so far. Truth, as open to human beings, ultimately rests on a fundamental accord of the human intellect with the divine intellect, which is the one that sustains and gives meaning to the being there of the thing, of the world out there. This is what might be called a prelapsarian view of the truth. It works well in paradise. But such an accord cannot explain by itself the archaic fear of the truth, fear of the inevitable sacred character of the truth. One can understand that if the fundamental accord were somehow broken, the result would be error, untruth, rather than truth. But where does the archaic fear come from? How did the luminosity of the original sacred, the shining disclosure, the unconcealment, the opening up of the being of the world-out-there to the eyes amazed of this new creature recently brought to the world of the spirit, how—we ask—did it all become the face of a threat, an irresistible prompting to look for a refuge?

This is where we need the help of René Girard's invaluable, irreplaceable contribution to our understanding of how violence infiltrated, so to speak, and took over, the realm of the sacred, of the spirit. Nobody has explained as thoroughly as he has the irreducible ambivalence of the archaic sacred: saving remedy and poison—good, indispensable, if expelled, if kept at a distance, but deadly if you touch it. Girard has taught us that violence, fratricidal human violence, is the very element of which the archaic sacred is made; that the archaic sacred is ultimately violence sacralized, violence made sacred in the very act of being expelled; or still, human violence transformed from bad and destructive to good, pacifying, foundational, as the violence of all against all becomes, mimetically and automatically, the violence of all against one. Girard has discovered the universal validity of Virgil's old prescription, *unum pro multis dabitur caput*[8] (one head will be given up for the sake of many). He has explained to us how "Satan expels Satan," to use Christ's terms. In other words, he has given us fundamental concepts such as the so-called scapegoat mechanism: the original mimetic crisis and its sacrificial, sacralizing resolution through the elimination of a totally arbitrary victim made unique, absolutely different from everybody and everything, sacred, by the violent unanimity that kills it.

The simplicity, the sheer elegance, and unparalleled explanatory power of the mimetic theory carried many of us along on a wave of enthusiasm. In time, however, some sensible questions were asked even among Girard's convinced followers. We owe some of these questions to the clear thinking and solid theological background of the late Father Raymund Schwager. For the fact is that, for a Judeo-Christian reader of the Bible, Girard's theory works perfectly on "fallen" human nature, in particular on city-founding human nature—that is to say, on Cain and his descendants, the *civitas terrena*. But it has nothing to say about paradise. It has exactly the opposite problem we have found in St. Thomas Aquinas. A problem to which Schwager alluded in his last book, *Banished from Eden: Original Sin and Evolutionary Theory in the Drama of Salvation*.[9] His view is that even though mimetic theory does not deal with prelapsarian innocence, it is not in principle opposed to accepting a real historical nucleus behind the mythical story of Adam and Eve in paradise:

> [We] can readily accept mythical and archetypal elements in ["the biblical story of origins"] and yet ascribe a historical nucleus to it. From this point of view, the details of how the events occurred remain, of course, hidden. . . . Nor does the mimetic interpretation oblige us to suppose that all evil was set in motion by one or two human beings who themselves had scarcely emerged from the animal realm. . . . However, since the mimetic theory accepts real events in its interpretation of myths, it holds that the same approach is appropriate in interpreting the biblical primal history. So all theological arguments whose point of departure is the original goodness of creation and which plead the cause of a fall as historical occurrence can once more obtain their full importance. (*Banished*, 27–28)

But, it seems to me, this is no longer in accord with the initial view of the sacrificial crisis and the victimage mechanism as nothing less than the missing link, the evolutionary passage from animal to man. Most of us believed initially that this passage could be explained in a totally naturalistic way. All that was needed was a gradual, purely biological increase in mimetism, which could be expected to occur with the growth of the brain, and which would alter the nature of internecine violence to the point where purely genetic, instinctual mechanisms of violence control would break down, and the victimage mechanism of all against one would automatically take over. The victim was seen as the first collective, social sign beyond the realm of genetic instinct. At which point, not only the human being as such was born, but also the sacred—the violent sacred, of course, a human invention entirely. It was no surprise when *Violence and the Sacred* was announced in *Le Monde* as "an atheistic explanation" of the sacred or of religion.[10]

In fact, to the best of my knowledge, this is still the thinking of Girard, in spite of Schwager's last book, which was first published in German in 1997. For example, this is how he responds to the interviewer Maria Stella Barberi, in *Celui par qui le scandale arrive*, who asks him if he is saying that humankind begins in violence.

> R. G.—Il n'y a pas d'autre homme que l'homme de la chute. Au début, c'est la chute. Je crois l'avoir déjà dit, le christianisme se rend visible de façon sacrificielle et c'est là son génie.[11]
>
> [There is no other man but the man of the fall. In the beginning was the fall. I think I have said it already, Christianity becomes visible in a sacrificial manner, and that is precisely its genius.]

I no longer believe that this is a tenable view within the parameters of the Christian revelation, even as explained by Girard himself. "In the beginning was the fall," says Girard in this particular text. The fall from what? Either there was no fall at all, or there was something before the fall. Furthermore, if we put it in the language of the Gospels, what Girard is saying here is that, as it concerns man, in the beginning was Satan. For, in Girard's theory, Satan is Christ's word for the spirit—that is to say, the internal logic of the victimage mechanism—and therefore also refers to the one who hides the truth, the "father of lies." In the beginning, then, was the big lie, the source of all lies. But how can the lie come before the truth? Either there was truth before the lie, or there was never any lie. But if there was never any lie, there was never any Satan. Does that mean, then, that Christ did not know what he was talking about? Girard cannot have it both ways. Either Christ is the ultimate root and authority on mimetic theory and sacrifice, as Girard has always maintained, or he is not, he is only a supporting historical authority for the rationality of the theory, which must stand on its own.[12]

In a still later text, one of his lectures on sacrifice given at the Bibliothèque Nationale de France in 2002, we read the following:

> Mimetic theory renders an account of sacrifice and archaic religion in terms of a purely natural force, human hypermimeticism. Because it exacerbates rivalries, this hypermimeticism destroys the dominance patterns in animal societies, but it replaces them, in the paroxysm of violence it releases, with another natural restraint: the mechanism of victimization, the founding murder that produces ritual sacrifice in its turn. In this genesis, there is not the slightest recourse to transcendence or to anything "irrational."
>
> The religious belief common to all archaic societies, . . . consists in thinking that the "miracle" of sacrifice, the minimal character of its violence, is too good to be true and so incomprehensible that it seems beyond natural explanation. They appeal therefore to an absolute, properly transcendent power beyond the human.[13]

I find this rather problematic, and at the same time unwittingly revealing. Why problematic? If the exponential increase in animal mimetism, if human "hypermimetism," is a purely natural, biological phenomenon leading automatically, in a totally unconscious way, to the victimage mechanism, or rather, since the word "victim" is inappropriate at this point, to the violent convergence of all against one, which suddenly brings a cessation of violence to the group, then at that point the purely natural biological process has reached its goal. It ends as soon as violence stops, except for its tendency, common to all life processes, to repeat itself in similar circumstances. Nature, pure biology, has nothing more to do or to say. The group, the horde, has survived for the moment. And we are still, at this point, dealing with an animal group that has randomly stumbled on a collectively generated mechanism of survival—an evolutionary improvement perhaps, but still an automatic mechanism for the temporary cessation of intraspecific violence, that is all.

In principle, this mechanism can be repeated indefinitely without altering anything fundamental about its animal character. Adding hundreds of thousands, or millions, of years ("L'évolution prend toujours le temps dont elle a besoin")[14] in principle does not change anything. Animals can continue to be animals forever. In reality, we have no idea at all what such an endless repetition of a collective mechanism of survival could produce, or the way it might or might not evolve within itself. We may conjecture ad infinitum, without ever reaching the specific point at which animal instinct turns into human spirit, at which the victim becomes not just a fact, a thing lying there, but a symbol, a revelation or manifestation of something beyond itself. We may, of course, reasonably conjecture a posteriori that such a point was indeed reached, but I do not think we can ever know exactly when that point was reached, or why then and not before or after. And because of that, neither can we know in a purely naturalistic way whether or not the victim was the first human symbol, the first to reveal the spirit, the meaningful being-there-ness of the world to human eyes. Faith, not natural science, tells us that such a revelation occurred before the violent crisis (even if it was, conceivably, only for an extremely short period). Faith also tells us that it was actually the violent crisis and its victimizing resolution that clouded everything, spoiling man's relation to nature, and distorting his vision of the world out there. It is indeed faith, Judeo-Christian faith, that tells us that it was the world out there, full of trees and all kinds of animals, inhabited by the spirit of God, that became the first symbol, the first meaningful being-there in the eyes of man.[15] And it tells us why: man saw what God saw, he saw it through God. In fact, according to Genesis 2:19–20, the Lord God brought all the wild animals, and the birds, and the cattle to man so that man would give each one its proper name. And "if we recall," says Pannenberg, "that for the archaic mind, the name of a thing is not something external to it but contains the nature of the thing itself, it becomes clear that this biblical passage says nothing less than that the human being, because of its participation in the divine Spirit, is capable of grasping the nature of things."[16]

But then hypermimetic man violently substituted another man, other fellow creatures, for God, and envious rivalry spiraled out of control, leading to the sacrificial crisis and the birth of all kinds of false gods in constant need of bloody victims.

Girard, of course, does not claim to know at what point the hypermimetic animal turned into a creature capable of conceiving such a thing as "omnipotence," even a "transcendent omnipotence." All he says is that it was the victimage mechanism that first revealed it to the creature; that is to say, it was the victimage mechanism that forced the creature to react that way. This is the way he put it in *Evolution and Conversion*: "At some stage of the evolutionary path—which turns primates into humans—a sort of prohibition of a religious nature or some sort of fear of an immense invisible power at the most basic level triggered prohibitions against violence."[17] Since that is the first encounter of the creature with the sacred, from then on we can safely call the creature a man, a human being. Thus original man, the most archaic man, imagined, invented this "omnipotence situated beyond the reach of man, properly transcendent," because he had no clue about how the sacrificial system worked. In the view of archaic man, "the 'miracle' of sacrifice was too unexpected and too incomprehensible to be susceptible of a 'natural explanation.'" If that is so, then indeed archaic man was onto something very important, because the "miracle" of sacrifice is in fact not "susceptible of [an exclusively] natural explanation." As I have been saying, I do not think that animal hypermimetism will ever get us to ritual sacrifice. Which brings up the problem of *méconnaissance*. Was archaic man as clueless as he appears to be in this text of Girard?

Let us pause for a moment. Archaic man, we are told, appeals to a made-up, imaginary, transcendent omnipotence, because he does not really know what is going on. We must assume, therefore, that if he knew, he would not imagine such a thing. At first sight this looks very much like the old argumentation that said that men created the gods to explain thunder, lightning, and other natural phenomena about which they had no clue. I grant, of course, that the similarity with the old argument, although not entirely out of place here, can only get us so far. It is rather superficial. Girard will tell us that this particular lack of knowledge in archaic man is not a historical accident: the very violence of the process in which they are engaged inevitably prevents them from finding out what is really going on. If they really knew, they would not do it, or rather, the sacrificial process would stop working for them. Therefore, the sacrificial process can only produce its beneficial effects on the basis of *méconnaissance*, of not knowing, or of misinterpreting, what is going on.

Nevertheless, there is a huge gap, a long distance, between not knowing what is going on and seeing the victim as the embodiment of an invisible, omnipotent power beyond the reach of man, of the group, the horde. How could this new creature over the face of the earth "explain" to himself this radically new phenomenon, in terms of an immensely powerful and invisible transcendence, unless he already had that mental possibility imprinted in his mind? If he had no notion whatsoever about God, how in the world could he possibly imagine a false god, a purely violent god? For that is what the "transcendent omnipotence" really is. Therefore, is this purely imaginary "transcendent omnipotence" not an argument in favor of the preexistence of the real thing and of a prelapsarian stage? Either there is no god at all, and everything is biology, or you have to begin with the true God. You simply cannot begin with a false god, and then have it evolve into the true One. Unless, of course, you want to say that Christ is an evolutionary result of the original violence-turned-god. Which I do not think for a moment is what Girard ever intended. Therefore, yes, there was *méconnaissance*, because there was also an underlying, fundamental *connaissance*.

Everything changes, however, if we start not with a prehuman, mimetic animal violently trapped in the middle of an unprecedented collective crisis, but already with a man, a human being. I agree with Gil Bailie:

> The first human did not have human parents. This statement, so simple, so logically incontrovertible, can serve to disabuse us of the crypto-Darwinian presuppositions with which our age and our thinking are suffused. However willing one might be to acknowledge the role of genetic adaptation in the development of organic life, it is an indisputable fact that the first human on earth did not have human parents. Our earliest ancestors appeared perhaps around 100 thousand years ago, but the important point is precisely the *point* at which hominization happened, for the transition from the non-human to the human occurred, as Claude Levi-Strauss put it, "at a single stroke."
>
> "Catholic theology affirms that the emergence of the first members of the human species (whether as individuals or in populations) represents an event that is not susceptible of a purely natural explanation and which can appropriately be attributed to divine intervention." So said the Catholic Church's International Theological Commission in 2004.[18]

This new human creature would be a hypermimetic one, to be sure, but one who already sees the world *and* his fellow creatures like no animal had ever seen them before. In the words of Schwager:

> The "fulguration" or the emergence by which they arose out of the animal realm (speaking scientifically), or the self-transcendence by which they became humans through the creative action of God (speaking theologically), would have led to opening up in them an utterly new feeling of immeasurable vastness with intensive emotional clarity. (*Banished from Eden*, 52)

At this point I am less interested in the subjective "feeling" of this new, but already human creature than in trying to imagine the "immeasurable vastness" that opens up before his and her eyes—awestruck and amazed, as we may well imagine. For this is the first time that a creature, a product, of this world sees it as true, as real, and therefore sees the spiritual dimension of the physical world out there. In fact, something extraordinarily important and consequential may have actually happened also inside the world, and not only inside the new creature, at that revealing moment. For the truth is not an accident of the world out there. It belongs to the essence of that world as it truly reveals itself to a human mind, not to a creature biologically trapped in a web of hypermimetic relations, unable, by definition, to see the reality of the world out there as such, as real.

But perhaps it was also at that revealing moment that the germ of the problem, the beginning of the fall, seeped in, mixed with the very amazement of those eyes. For they were looking not only at the world out there, but also (and, we must assume, with equal amazement) at their fellow creatures. And the question is, how could this amazement in the very face of the truth—that is to say, of that which is *truly* out there—not be also at the root of the "hypermimetism" of the new creature? Girard has taught us from the beginning, in *Mensonge romantique et vérité romanesque*, that specifically human desire is fundamentally "meta-physical." Hypermimetism is ultimately a desire for the very being of the model and rival. There is clearly something spiritual about human rivalry, something beyond animality. Even though it may lead to a catastrophic loss of freedom, to a hellish kind of slavery, human violence is the violence of a free creature, precisely because it is open-ended, the kind of violence capable of reaching the paroxysmal intensity of the sacrificial crisis. If this is so, it seems to me that it makes more sense to start with the spirit, with the truth of the world out there, which in a perverted way is turned into the energy that drives the violence to its victimizing limit, rather than to try to derive the spirit from a purely biological process. I do not think it is correct to say that beyond a certain biologically grounded mimetic threshold the hominid creature automatically turns into a human being. I think it had to be the other way around: the newly found, the newly created, spirit drove the biological mimetic process far beyond its natural boundaries.

In my view, the archaic sacred, the violent sacred, is not a biological process taken to its limit. It is a perversion of the true sacred, that is to say, of the spirit, the "immeasurable vastness," that sustains the truth of what is *truly* out there. And I think that archaic man knew it in his own way when he sacralized his own hypermimetic violence, when he saw it as "an absolute, properly transcendent power beyond the human." In fact, I think we can say about the sacred something similar to what we say about physical energy: human beings can neither create nor destroy the sacred, they can only transform it. The original, spontaneous victimage mechanism, and its sacralizing resolution, was the first human transformation of the sacred. And it is important to realize that even in the midst of such a paroxysmal violence, the spirit was still there. Which I think also makes sense from a theological point of view: Christ was already there when the first spontaneously generated victim was killed, which could hardly be the case if there was nothing "transcendental" about the process, if Satan were simply the result of biological evolution.[19]

Girard would be the first to admit that what makes his own theory historically possible is the Christian text. This is why he has openly and repeatedly acknowledged that he has not discovered anything that was not already there in the very text of the Gospels. It is Christ who ultimately reveals the sacrificial, the foundational, character of human violence: the way human beings delude themselves by and about their own violence. And He can do it because He has no part in it. He is completely outside the scandalizing mechanism that triggers and sustains the open-ended violent reciprocity among human beings. Nevertheless, Christ's injunction to hypermimetic human beings is not to stop being mimetic, but to be mimetic the right way, His way: "Imitate me as I imitate the Father." God Himself is mimetic. To the extent that one may perhaps speak of God's desire, is His desire, His love for man, not the supreme example of mimetic desire? A desire that moves Him to become man, to take on the being of man, to abandon Himself into the hands of man? When St. Paul says, "I have made myself a slave to all . . . I have become all things to all men, that I might by all means save some" (1 *Cor.*

9:19–22), he is imitating Christ: "Be imitators of me, as I am of Christ" (11:1). How could man's "hypermimetic" desire, *qua* desire, be anything other than a pale reflection, a clouded image, of God's supreme mimesis? Therefore, reciprocal, rivalry-driven, hypermimetic human violence can only be seen, from a Christian perspective, as a perverse, satanic distortion, a falsification, of preexisting God's loving mimesis. And the possibility of such a distortion as such, as a distortion, must be posited at the very beginning. From a Christian perspective, mimetic human violence is a *fall* from, and a rejection of, preexisting God's loving mimesis.

The serpent told the woman, "You shall be like gods," if they ate of the fruit. But, as Girard has pointed out, what the serpent neglected to say is that they would be like gods to one another; that if God is ignored, your neighbor steps in His place, becoming your model and, inevitably, sooner or later, your rival. If God is ignored, the mimetic crisis is only a matter of time. This is clearly as relevant today as it was in the beginning. But perhaps we have less of an excuse today than they had then. For the difference between gods and men must have been far less pronounced, far less distinct in the beginning. The "immeasurable vastness" that the spirit opened up must have included everything and everybody rather evenly. For that very reason, the horror of the hypermimetic sacrificial crisis penetrated everything. Truth itself, the spiritual, the meaningful dimension of the world out there, became a profound source of anxiety and fear, an ever-present threat against which being human meant finding a defense, a refuge. And this is the background that gives greater significance to Auerbach's basic intuition about the two different and fundamental approaches to the representation of reality in Western literature, the Homeric and the biblical. Behind such a representation of reality lies a "toute-puissance," to use Girard's words, "an overwhelming power," to use a biblical expression, with which the narrator has to deal before he can represent anything.

CHAPTER 1

Auerbach's *Mimesis* Revisited

Let us begin with Auerbach's description of what he called "the basic impulse of the Homeric style":

> To represent phenomena in a fully externalized form, visible and palpable in all their parts, and completely fixed in their spatial and temporal relations. Nor do psychological processes receive any other treatment: here too nothing must remain hidden and unexpressed . . . a continuous rhythmic procession of phenomena passes by, and never is there a form left fragmentary or half-illuminated, never a lacuna, never a gap, never a glimpse of unplumbed depths.
>
> And this procession of phenomena takes place in the foreground—that is, in a local and temporal present which is absolute. (6–7)[1]

The view, therefore, is that of a very detailed picture laid out on a flat and perfectly smooth surface, which can be stretched horizontally in every direction, but offers no inkling of anything that may lie underneath or beyond. In other words, complete superficiality—even though the superficiality of Homer's style is not a formal defect, but, on the contrary, the very perfection of its form, what it is meant to be. Because everything is visible, everything is surface.[2]

The episode chosen by Auerbach as typical of this style, the recognition by the old nurse Eurykleia of Odysseus's scar, is both striking and, fittingly, quite long. But there are many other shorter examples just as telling. For instance, it takes almost ten lines to describe Penelope's opening of the door to the chamber where Odysseus's bow is kept:

> *When she, shining among women, had come to the chamber,*
> *and had come up to the oaken threshold, which the carpenter*
> *once had expertly planed and drawn it true to a chalkline,*
> *and fitted the door posts to it and joined on the shining door leaves,*
> *first she quickly set the fastening free of the hook, then*
> *she inserted the key and knocked the bolt upward, pushing*
> *the key straight in, and the door bellowed aloud, as a bull*
> *does, when he feeds in his pasture; such was the noise the splendid*
> *doors made, struck with the key, and now they quickly spread open.*
>
> (21:42–50)[3]

Clearly, the Homeric poet must feel that he would not be doing his job properly if he simply said that Penelope opened the door and went in. The contrast with the biblical style could not be more striking. The biblical narrative is full of gaps and conspicuous silences. The story chosen by Auerbach, that of Abraham's sacrifice of Isaac, is perhaps the best possible example:

> The King James version translates the opening as follows (Genesis 22:1): "And it came to pass after these things, that God did tempt Abraham, and said to him, Abraham! And he said, Behold, here I am." Even this opening startles us when we come to it from Homer. Where are the two speakers? We are not told. . . . Whence does [God] come? Whence does he call Abraham? We are not told. He does not come, like Zeus or Poseidon, from the Aethiopians, where he has been enjoying a sacrificial feast. . . . [If] we now turn to the other person in the dialogue, to Abraham. Where is he? We do not know . . . whether in Beersheba or elsewhere, whether indoors or in the open air, is not stated; it does not interest the narrator . . . ; and what Abraham was doing when God called him is left in the same obscurity. . . .

> After this opening . . . the story itself begins . . . it unrolls with no episodes in a few independent sentences whose syntactical connection is of the most rudimentary sort. In this atmosphere it is unthinkable that an implement, a landscape through which the travelers passed, the serving-men, or the ass, should be described. . . . They are serving-men, ass, wood, and knife, and nothing else, without an epithet; they are there to serve the end which God has commanded; what in other respects they were, are, or will be, remains in darkness. . . .
>
> They began "early in the morning." But at what time on the third day did Abraham lift his eyes and see his goal? The text says nothing on the subject. . . . So "early in the morning" is given, not as an indication of time, but for the sake of its ethical significance; it is intended to express the resolution, the promptness, the punctual obedience of the sorely tried Abraham. Bitter to him is the early morning in which he saddles his ass, calls his serving-men and his son Isaac, and sets out; but he obeys. (8–10)

Not only individual episodes, but the composition of the Old Testament as a whole is also full of gaps or discontinuities. "[It] is incomparably less unified than the Homeric poems." However, "the greater the separateness and horizontal disconnection . . . the stronger is their general vertical connection . . . which is entirely lacking in Homer" (17).

It is precisely through these discontinuities, or these episodic gaps, that the invisible dimension of historical reality filters in, that a sense of depth and background is conveyed, and a profound concern for essential truth beyond the empirical details is communicated at all levels. Even at the psychological level, "the great figures of the Old Testament are so much more fully developed, so much more fraught with their own biographical past, so much more distinct as individuals, than are the Homeric heroes" (17). In other words, these characters have a history; the old man of today is no longer the person he was in his youth. In contrast, the "life-histories" of Homeric heroes "are clearly set forth once and for all"; even Odysseus, who goes through so many events for such a long time, "on his return is exactly the same as he was when he left Ithaca two decades earlier. But what a road, what a fate, lie between the Jacob who cheated his father out of his blessing and the old man whose favorite son has been torn to pieces by a wild beast" (17). Circumstances, and above all, the will of God, change and mold the biblical characters. "Indeed generally, this element of development gives the Old Testament stories a historical character, even when the subject is purely legendary and traditional." This is also why, as opposed to Homer, who "remains within the legendary with all his material . . . the Old Testament comes closer and closer to history as the narrative proceeds" (18–19). It is as if anything that the Homeric style touches becomes legend, regardless of its historical or ontological status, and the opposite happens with the biblical style: even if the material is legendary, it acquires the flavor of history. It is there because it is felt to be true. Therefore, in reference to the truth in general, the perfectly illuminated, the smooth and detailed surface of the Homeric text acts as a barrier, a blind. The homogeneous and unbroken surface is precisely what prevents us from seeing through or beyond it, or, to put it differently, what prevents a sense of the importance of the real as such, as that which is true, from filtering through and giving density to the representation of the facts of reality. The multiplication of visible surface details stretching in every horizontal direction turns everything into what Dante would have called *parlare fabuloso.*[4] In fact, the glaring surface of the facts is so consistent, so evenly extended, and its contrast with the Bible, a text of similar antiquity, so striking that not only must we suspect that the Homeric text has no interest in revealing anything behind the facts, but it appears rather likely on this evidence alone that it actually wants to hide that which it does not reveal. But why? That is what we want to reflect on.

Everybody, I assume, would agree that Homer is much closer to modern fiction than the Bible. And one might think that even from a fictional perspective, Homer's mythical text could have fabricated its own poetic sense of depth, could have striven for a transcendent truth beyond the surface of the myth. According to Auerbach, there is none of that in Homer, and I agree. He clings to the surface and holds our attention there, ignoring anything beyond the literal text itself. Never a reflective pause to divert our attention to wider or deeper considerations. Its brief meditations can hardly be called such:

> The general considerations which occasionally occur (. . . for example, v. 360: that in misfortune men age quickly) reveal a calm acceptance of the basic facts of human existence, but with no compulsion to brood over them, still less any passionate impulse to rebel against them or embrace them in an ecstasy of submission. (14)

But while one can understand a "calm acceptance" of the facts of life in the case of "aging quickly in misfortune," or something similar, such calm becomes surprising, even startling, when we find it in the midst of incredible violence. I am referring to Homer's famous narrative equilibrium in the midst of battle. War is war, and death is death, and sufferings are evenly distributed. He does not incline toward the Greeks or the Trojans, for example. He does not judge. He narrates the "wars of men," he does not take part in them. He laments them, just like the tragic chorus of a later time would lament the inexorable development of the tragic action, but with even more equanimity, just the facts. Does that mean that he is indifferent or unconcerned about such facts? Of course not, but it seems to be essential to the Homeric poem not to look behind the facts, not to generalize—just the facts, horrific as they may be sometimes. And, of course, this absence of a deeper or a more general level, this presentation of the facts as nothing but facts, leaves unanswered the question about the truth of those facts. Did they really happen or not? Homer does not say.

The gaps and discontinuities in the biblical text "startle" us, says Auerbach, when we come to it from Homer. And we should be so "startled." They are so unexpected. There is nothing in Homer to prepare us for what we find in the Bible. From a Homeric perspective, the Bible is indeed a strange text. But should we not wonder equally about the conspicuously homogeneous, gapless surface in Homer, about its blinding visibility? Looking at it with biblical eyes, it should appear no less strange, perhaps even scandalous. The reason why it does not look so strange to us is simply that we look at it through the prism of modern literary fiction. But that in itself can be seriously misleading. For even though modern literary fiction is a direct descendant of Homer, the distance between the two is quite great. When we read modern fiction, we do something that a Homeric Greek could not do, or at least not as casually and without thinking as we do it today: to bracket historical reality, historical truth, the reality of the world out there, and put it aside for the time being while we immerse ourselves in a world of make-believe. We do not deny that reality, the truth out there. We do not try to hide it. We simply suspend it for convenience's sake, push it out of sight temporarily. Fiction, we say, creates its own ad hoc reality with its own poetic truth. In fact, we may even think that such a poetic truth can reveal things, truthful things, about true reality.

To a Homeric Greek, this convenient, unproblematic separation between make-believe and true reality, this reassuring distance, was either not available, or not fully comprehensible. His relationship with the truth, with the real world out there, was far more problematic and infinitely more ambiguous. He could not just ignore it. He could imitate it, and he could fictionalize it. But in either case it was something he did to it or because of it, not something independent of it. He did not create a separate reality having nothing to do with the true one. He manipulated or disguised true reality, and this manipulation or disguising, which drew a veil over the real thing, was quite openly called lying—because a lie was still a lie, poetic or otherwise. Nobody had any problem with calling Homer a liar. What happened is that lying and divine inspiration were by no means antagonistic concepts. This is why, to a Homeric Greek, "[knowing] how to say many false things that were like true sayings"[5] was still an awe-inspiring, sacred art, which could not be approached lightly. Of course, that also meant that even though a lie was a lie, not all lies were equally admissible. Only divinely inspired lies were to be revered, lies conceived within a religious, quasi-ritual context. Strange as it may sound to modern ears, it was precisely the sacred character or association of the lie that turned it from something bad into something revered and required.[6] Homer's poetic lying was likewise a heroic art, Odysseus's art—"long-enduring" Odysseus, "resourceful," "crafty," "devious." This is how Athene describes her protégé:

> It would be a sharp one, and a stealthy one, who would ever get past you
> in any contriving; even if it were a god against you.
> You wretch, so devious, never weary of tricks, then you would not
> even in your own country give over your ways of deceiving
> and your thievish tales. They are near to you in your very nature.
> . . .
> [You] are [also] far the best of all mortal
> men for counsel and stories.[7]

That is the soul of the Homeric style. In essence, Homer's tale is Odysseus's tale. Of the two great Homeric heroes, Achilles and Odysseus, only the latter is made to perform like a poet, a narrator of tales. To celebrate Odysseus is to celebrate his narrative style and skill, which is not precisely that of telling the truth, but quite the opposite. Odysseus was renowned for his cunning in disguising, masking, the truth. He is, par excellence, the great disguiser. We must remember, the Trojan horse was his idea. What is important in his style, therefore, is how one positions oneself before the truth at any given moment. It is ultimately a matter of strategy. The obvious question is, should we not take Odysseus's cunning, his skill in masking the truth, as a clue to our approach to the *Odyssey* and, by extension, to Homer's style in general?

But Odysseus's tale is not just any tale in Western culture. It has an archetypal value. It is one of the pillars of a millenarian tradition, as Auerbach so brilliantly saw. In other words, it touches the foundation of such a tradition. Therefore, when we speak about Odysseus's hiding of the truth, we are not speaking about something accidental, or a reaction to a particular historical manifestation of the truth, but about his fundamental approach to truth as such, at its most basic ontological and existential level: the truth embodied in the reality of the world out there in the very act of being there, appearing to human eyes; truth as a metaphysical quality or dimension of the human world—that is to say, of the reality, both physical and cultural, inhabited by human beings. Because, as we anticipated in the Introduction, to human beings, physical reality is never just physical as it manifests itself as such, as reality, as that which is *truly out there*. Truth changes the character of the physical world. Or perhaps I should say that truth changes the way in which the world out there *is out there* for human beings.[8] This must also be why the "artistic" representation of reality is such a uniquely human characteristic. "Artistic" representation is probably the clearest testimony to the transcendental visibility of the truth in the empirical reality of the human habitat. "Man dwells as a poet on this earth,"[9] said Heidegger in his commentary on a poem by Hölderlin. It is the truth of what is *truly out there* that man wants to capture, to represent either in visible signs or in words. Animals, on the other hand, although they communicate with one another, do not speak, because they have absolutely nothing to say. Their world is not sayable. Of course, as soon as the truth of what is *truly* there is captured, re-presented (in its most primitive version—in cave paintings, for example—this existential "capture" would probably have to be understood rather literally, magically), it will no longer be that which *is truly out there*. A gap, a symbolic gap, a cultural space, will open up. This is the space of the sacred, the original human space[10]—which, if we are to judge by Homer's inspired representation of it, is, or has become at some point, a very ambiguous space, the breeding ground of the revered sacred lie, which so upset Plato against the poets, for example.

One notices that animals living in the wild are always vigilant, very much on guard against dangers lurking in their physical environment. In the case of human beings it was not the physical environment as such, in its materiality, that threatened them in a fundamental sense, but its sacred character, its metaphysical link to the truth, its transcendence. And such a fundamental threat, lurking everywhere but nowhere in particular, hovering over everything like an evil spirit, only makes sense anthropologically as a result of the sacrificial violence that took over, that usurped, the place of the true spirit. And is that not precisely the origin of the existential anxiety, or dread, or uneasiness, or *malaise*, of which Western philosophy has been speaking for almost two hundred years—Kierkegaard's "anxiety," for example, or that of Heidegger's in *Being and Time*?

> *That in the face of which one has anxiety is Being-in-the-world as such. . . .* That in the face of which one has anxiety is not an entity within-the-world. . . . Anxiety does not know what that in the face of which it is anxious is. . . . Therefore that which threatens . . . is already "there," and yet nowhere; it is so close that it is oppressive and stifles one's breath, and yet it is nowhere.[11]

The overwhelming power, the "omnipotence," of sacralized human violence is, theologically speaking, the immediate result of original sin, which, in a Girardian context, is the mimetic substitution of the human model/rival for God. In other words, mimetic theory does provide a convincing anthropological explanation for the otherwise unexplained anxiety that modern philosophy discovers in the fundamental constitution of the human being. Theology had already found its explanation in the very concept of original sin as an original choice of that which is human over God.

To repeat, the most archaic human attitude for which we can find anthropological evidence was not one of confidence and trust before the world out there. That world, in its very being-there, spoke of something unspeakable, revealed its truth as that which had to be concealed. A secret and dangerous truth, which could only be approached by taking extraordinary sacred precautions. At the very least, the primitive prudent thing was never to meet the truth with an open face, but always in disguise, from behind a mask.

A good tale, craftily woven, could be such a mask. Of course, a crafty tale can make use of a true story just as effectively as one that "tells many false things that look like true sayings," if it serves its overall strategic purpose of diverting attention from the truth. The only important thing is to have the necessary cunning to know when to tell one or the other, or a combination of both, as the sacred Heliconian muses told Hesiod: "We know how to speak many false things as though they were true; but we know, when we will, to utter true things."[12] Clearly we are worlds apart from something like Tasso's humble apology to the heavenly Muse, at the beginning of the *Gerusalemme liberata*, for adorning the truth with fictional delights.[13]

One can either hide oneself from the truth, or hide the truth from view, put it under cover. The latter option—that is, the poetic, the crafty one—may only be a ritual reenactment of the first. To hide the truth of what is real underneath the perfect, unbroken visibility of what is unreal, is just an artificial way of hiding oneself from the truth. Homer does create a poetic make-believe reality, but not for its own sake, and certainly not only to pass the time, as Auerbach thought. Homer is trying to hide something; that is to say, to hide from something at the very core of historical reality, something that attaches inexorably to the existential experience of the real as such, as that which is visibly out there—in other words, the truth. The fundamental problem faced by Homer found expression in Heraclitus's *Fragment 16*: "How can one hide before that which never sets?" If that which never sets, which stands in the light, unconcealed, is the truth (*aletheia*), its sacred shining, its being-there in whatever is there in the human habitat, clearly posed a problem and created an urgent task: that of hiding it from view, of protecting oneself from it.[14] But this is what Auerbach said:

> [The Homeric heroes] bewitch us and ingratiate themselves to us until we live with them in the reality of their lives; so long as we are reading or hearing the poems, it does not matter whether we know that all this is only legend, "make-believe." The oft-repeated reproach that Homer is a liar takes nothing from his effectiveness, he does not need to base his story on historical reality, his reality is powerful enough in itself; it ensnares us, weaving its web around us, and that suffices him. And this "real" world into which we are lured, exists for itself, contains nothing but itself; the Homeric poems conceal nothing, they contain no teaching

> and no secret second meaning. Homer can be analyzed . . . but he cannot be interpreted. (13)

Unwittingly this statement is an excellent confirmation of what we are trying to say. Auerbach sounds very much like a modern version of the ideal reader demanded by Homer: a reader seduced, "lured" into, "ensnared" by the Homeric song. For such a song intends to give the impression that that is all there is. This is why Homer can indeed be considered the father of all modern fiction. Auerbach's response echoes uncritically the most profound meaning and intention of the Homeric song. Except for an important detail. The poetic charm, the attraction of the "make-believe," works on us, says Auerbach, "so long as we are reading or hearing the poems." What happens, then, after we close the book or leave the auditorium? Will the poem be remembered simply as an interesting, even brilliant, poetic exercise, which kept us charmed for a while before returning to some serious business in the real world? This may very well be what happens in the case of a modern reader ("merely to make us forget our own reality for a few hours," 15). But I think that Auerbach is wrong to imply that that could also be the situation with the original audience. For the original audience would inevitably associate the charm of the song with the great heroic charmer celebrated in it, Odysseus himself, for whom the crafty, "artistic" manipulation of the truth was a matter of survival, of "long enduring" through countless sufferings and close encounters with a harsh destiny. For in terms of a capacity for enchanting and seducing the listener, Odysseus is as good as Homer, and Homer as good as Odysseus. Here is a vivid example of how Odysseus could charm his listener, as reported by Eumaios, the swineherd, who still does not know that the stranger who talked to him was his master in disguise. He is reporting to Penelope:

> *Such stories he tells, he would charm out the dear heart within you.*
> *Three nights I had him with me, and for three days I detained him*
> *in my shelter, for he came first to me. He had fled from a vessel;*
> *but he has not yet told the story of all his suffering.*
> *But as when a man looks to a singer, who has been given*
> *from the gods the skill with which he sings for delight of mortals,*
> *and they are impassioned and strain to hear it when he sings to them,*
> *so he enchanted me in the halls as he sat beside me.* (17:514–21)

Odysseus's audience listens to him as it listens to a god-like singer. He keeps them all "impassioned . . . straining to hear." His song-like tale keeps them "enchanted." Which is exactly what Homer does with his audience: witness Auerbach's perceptive observation. Not only is Homer's story Odysseus's story, Homer's art is Odysseus's art. Which means that this "lure," this "snare," this poetic cocoon that the crafty narrator "webs around us," is not an innocent byproduct, a mere psychological effect caused by disinterested artistic beauty or craftsmanship. The very words used by the perceptive reader Auerbach, or the enchanted listener Eumaios powerfully suggest that there is nothing disinterested about it. It is a deliberate diversion, a strategic feint—in other words, a defense mechanism against "that which never sets," the threatening truth, the reality, of the world out there. It is a shield against a sacred and all-powerful destiny, which it would be foolish for a human being to trust, rather than to avoid or to appease. Once again, the very words "lure," "snare," etc., do not seem to be compatible with, or faithful to, the notion of "disclosure," "unconcealment," "rescuing from forgetfulness" implied in the word *aletheia*. Although even this devious response to the truth, as we have already indicated, bears witness implicitly to its metaphysical or sacred shining, for it is specifically a response to it. What this means is that ultimately, it is not so much we, the audience, that Odysseus or Homer are trying to "enchant," to "ensnare," but truth itself, the reality of a world that is *truly* out there menacingly, that appears in the light of the truth, but whose appearing is anything but reassuring. The Homeric audience is, of course, "enchanted"; they are indeed "impassioned and strain to hear." But that only means that they join in the performance, at least in spirit. They participate in the "ensnaring" of the truth, a task that is as important to them as it is for the singer himself. They participate in the poetic performance, just like the sacrificing community participates in the ritual sacrifice being offered *for* them, on their behalf, by the sacrificer. Modern fiction, on the other hand, is what remains after all the ritual echoes have disappeared from the stories, and they have just become mere desacralized entertainment. That is the moment at which Auerbach observes and analyzes the Homeric text.

We should insist on this. Homer's proximity to the ritual is the chasm that separates his world from ours. To him, as well as to his audience, a hero was a quasi-divine figure. We must remember that the hero cult was a well-established practice in Greek civilization: "the evidence for it goes back at least as far as the 'Geometric' period of the first millennium B.C.E."[15] In fact, according to Gregory Nagy, "the Panhellenic Epos is the product of the same era that produced an upsurge in local hero cults."[16] And, of course, no cult without ritual sacrifice, which is always at the center of any kind of worship, and a constant presence throughout the *Iliad* and the *Odyssey*.

The poetic entrapment, the "ensnaring," of the truth must have had a long, sacred tradition behind it. It is still present in the archetypical cunning wisdom of Odysseus. But it is no longer there for us. For we are not only heirs to the Greeks, but also to Jerusalem and the Bible, and perhaps nowhere is this more relevant than in our relation to the truth, to the real as true. We can be afraid of the truth in any particular case under specific circumstances. But being fundamentally afraid of the truth as such, as that which reveals reality, being-there-ness, to human eyes, as that "which never sets," is almost incomprehensible to us. And yet, this is precisely what we have to understand if we want to understand Homer's hiding of the truth under his poetic, seamless surface. Fiction, the deceiving truth—which is nothing but truth diverted, bypassed, deceived—had for him an existential significance, the depth of which remains beyond the reach or the scope of our modern glorification of the arts as basically disinterested activity. There was nothing disinterested in Homer's poetic "make-believe."

It is not a question of the Homeric poems containing some sort of "secret second meaning." In this sense, Auerbach was right. I do not think there is any such thing in Homer. There is concealment, though. But we could actually say that Homer conceals in plain view. There is nothing underneath the make-believe surface except the deepest hope and desire that such a make-believe surface may be sufficient to keep the real thing at bay, that the fiction may stand in lieu of reality. In other words, the deepest hope and desire that reality itself, the truth, may take the bait, so to speak, fall in the trap of the perfectly smooth and visible surface. Auerbach sees the narrative result, but misinterprets the intention behind it.

> It is all very different in the Biblical stories [says Auerbach]. Their aim is not to bewitch the senses, and if nevertheless they produce lively sensory effects, it is only because the moral, religious, and psychological phenomena which are their sole concern are made concrete in the sensible matter of life. But their religious intent involves an absolute claim to historical truth.

> . . . [The] Biblical narrator, the Elohist, had to believe in the objective truth of the story of Abraham's sacrifice—the existence of the sacred ordinances of life rested upon the truth of this and similar stories. He had to believe in it passionately; or else (as many rationalistic interpreters believed and perhaps still believe) he had to be a conscious liar—no harmless liar like Homer, who lied to give pleasure, but a political liar with a definite end in view, lying in the interest of a claim to absolute authority.
>
> To me, the rationalistic interpretation seems psychologically absurd; but even if we take it into consideration, the relation of the Elohist to the truth of his story still remains a far more passionate and definite one than is Homer's relation. . . . What he produced, then, was not primarily oriented toward "realism" (if he succeeded in being realistic, it was a means, not an end); it was oriented toward truth. . . . ; without believing in Abraham's sacrifice, it is impossible to put the narrative of it to the use for which it was written. Indeed, we must go even further. The Bible's claim to truth is not only far more urgent than Homer's, it is tyrannical—it excludes all other claims. The world of the Scripture stories is not satisfied with claiming to be a historically true reality—it insists that it is the only real world, is destined for autocracy. . . .
>
> Let no one object that this goes too far, that not the stories, but the religious doctrine, raises the claim to absolute authority; because the stories are not, like Homer's, simply narrated "reality." Doctrine and promise are incarnate in them and inseparable from them; for that very reason they are fraught with "background" and mysterious, containing a second, concealed meaning. (14–15)

Before we proceed to comment on what Auerbach is saying here directly about the Bible, we may notice also what his words tell us indirectly about his view of Homer. He establishes here a radical contrast between Homer's text and the Bible on the basis of religion. The Bible is clearly a sacred text, a religious text. Homer's poem—Auerbach takes for granted—is not. This, it seems to me, is the underlying reason why he cannot really believe that Homer's relationship to the truth can be serious, or even important, while on the other hand, he has no problem at all in understanding that the Bible is vitally interested in the truth of what it says. The reason is clear: "the existence of the sacred ordinances of life rested on it."

But he is making an unwarranted assumption, as we anticipated in the Introduction. He assumes that religion, by definition, trusts and defends the historical, objective truth of what it says or practices. Since clearly this is not the case with Homer, Auerbach assumes that Homer's text has no religious implications, nothing to do with "the sacred ordinances of life." It is "simply narrated 'reality'" to keep us "enchanted" for a while. But we have already seen that the sacred character of the truth does not necessarily call for allegiance. Quite the contrary: there is such a thing as being interested in hiding the truth. And such is the case in most primitive societies, where secrecy and truth are intertwined notions. This is why we can learn much about primitive religion from Homer. Historically and socially, it is impossible to isolate Homer's text from the religious practices of his day. Failure to recognize that is a serious flaw in Auerbach's analysis. How could a text of such cultural importance and centrality as Homer's was, existing in an old and thoroughly religious society, have nothing (or nothing important) to do with religion? "Divine" Homer was not just another epic bard. "To the ancient Greeks, Homer enjoyed a reputation as something between Holy Writ and an encyclopedia of universal knowledge," says Whitman.[17] The *Iliad* and the *Odyssey* were central to the education of Athenian citizens: "To be a Greek was to be educated," says Walter Burkert, "and the foundation of all education was Homer."[18] But above all we have the testimony of the poems themselves, which are saturated, so to speak, with the presence of the sacred. It does not matter that the Homeric gods are rather fanciful creations. It was not Homer who created them. They were an integral part of very old popular beliefs and ritual practices. They gave expression to the deeply felt and ubiquitous presence of the sacred in Greek society. "Everything is filled with gods," said Thales. Therefore, if "it is impossible to put the [biblical] narrative to the use for which it was written," unless one believes in its objective truth, should we not ask the same question about Homer's treatment of the truth in its relation to the sacrificial practices of his time, which formed the core of his religion? How did Homer's "narrated reality" fit in with classical pagan religion? The same question emerges also from the following quote:

> It will . . . be said that [the biblical style] is to be explained by the particular concept of God which the Jews held and which was wholly different from that of the Greeks. True enough—but this constitutes no objection. For

> how is the Jewish concept of God to be explained? . . . The concept of God held by the Jews is less a cause than a symptom of their manner of comprehending and representing things. (8)

If the "Homeric style" is a good example of the Greek "manner of comprehending and representing things," should we not also assume that the Greek concept of divinity, of the sacred, may be a symptom of their Homeric way of facing up to the world? But since the Greek concept of the sacred is not embodied in a set of doctrines and beliefs, but rather in a complex network of ritual sacrificial practices, how do such practices relate to the "Homeric style," or vice versa? This question will have to be addressed in due course. But there is a more immediate one now.

If the concept of God is to be explained by the manner of comprehending and representing things, how is this manner, in turn, to be explained? We could continue to beg this question over and over indefinitely. However, the point I have been trying to make is that, in the end, in the final analysis—or what amounts to the same thing, in the beginning, originally—you cannot separate these two things, the sacred and the "manner of comprehending and representing things." The sacred is the alpha point of all human "manner of comprehending and representing things," those things that are *truly* there, and that manifest themselves to human eyes in and beyond their physical reality. They manifest themselves as sacred, or in a sacred way. They, in their physical being there, bear the imprint, appear in the light, of something physically invisible, something beyond themselves. To the best of our knowledge, there is nothing in the human world older than its sacred dimension. Empirical reality reveals the sacred to human eyes in its being there, a new way of being there, different from anything that existed before. As far as human beings are concerned, in the beginning was the sacred. There is no other existential contact with the world, no other "manner of comprehending and representing things," more original than the originally sacred contact—which is much more than just a contact, it is a relationship. This is as true for the Jews as for the Greeks, of course. This originally sacred contact with the world does not carry with it necessarily any particular conception of God, or even of the existence of such a thing as an individualized divinity separate and independent from the reality out there. It simply means that the new reality draws the attention of the human being in an unprecedented way—in a way that goes beyond or apart from any utilitarian or instinctual need that the human being may share with other animals. In this original sense, we can accept Auerbach's proposition that "the concept of God . . . is less a cause than a symptom of [the] manner of comprehending and representing things." Because such a concept, although it is a historical development, is already there in germ, *in potentia*, as soon as a human being "comprehends and represents" something. Why this original sacred germ developed historically into the concept of God that we find in the Bible, we do not really know, anthropologically speaking. But it is important to realize that no concept of God can develop from something that is not already sacred. Only the sacred generates the sacred. As we have already indicated, human beings can only transform the sacred in the course of history. It is equally important to realize that such a history is also the history of the relationship between the human creature and the sacred in the reality out there. It is at this developmental, historical level that profound differences appear among different concepts of God or, in a more general sense, of the sacred.

In the case at hand, the most obvious and fundamental difference between the human relationship with the sacred in the Bible and in Homer is that the Bible trusts the sacred and, therefore, the truth, the reality of what is *truly* there, and Homer does not. He, like Odysseus, finds it dangerously unpredictable. Although it would be more accurate to say that the figure, the character, of Odysseus emerges out of the living experience of such unpredictability. It is the human face of it. Its name is Odysseus, the congenital, inspired liar, if we are to believe the words of his divine helper Athene.

At the opposite end we have, for example, the words of the Psalmist who glorifies in the fact that he walks "in the ways," or in "the law," of the Lord:

> *Blessed are those whose way is blameless,*
> *who walk in the law of the Lord!* (Psalm 119:1)

Because the law of the Lord, His commandments, are more than doctrine, more than a set of language utterances. They have a clear ontological status. They are the law of the universe; they rule the reality out there:

> *Open my eyes, that I may behold*
> *wondrous things out of your law.*

> *I am a sojourner on earth;*
> *hide not your commandments from me!*
> . . . .
> *Make me understand the way of your precepts,*
> *and I will meditate on your wondrous works.*
> . . . .
> *The earth, O Lord, is full of your steadfast love;*
> *teach me your statutes!*
> . . . .
> *Teach me good judgment and knowledge,*
> *for I believe in your commandments.*
> . . . .
> *all your commandments are true.*
> *Long have I known from your testimonies*
> *that you have founded them for ever.*
> . . . .
> *The sum of your word is truth;*
> *and every one of your righteous ordinances*
> *endures for ever.* (Psalm 119:18–160)

Which brings us to the question of the "tyrannical" character of the biblical claim to truth, according to Auerbach. I think what happened is that since the critic saw nobody claiming to be telling the truth, except the Bible, he thereby concluded that such a claim "excludes all other claims." The problem with this view, of course, is that there are no other competing claims. If Homer is the typical example of other nonbiblical narratives, we can see where the problem lies: not only does he not advance any claim to the truth, as Auerbach himself acknowledges, he does not want to; he is trying his best to avoid any direct encounter with the truth.

Whether or not we believe in the historical objectivity of the Bible, we must admit that it is the only narrative explicitly, "passionately" interested in the truth; the only one that wants to tell the whole truth and nothing else contrary to the truth. If the biblical story is a myth, it is a myth like no other—a myth that claims to be much more than a myth, and that, in itself, is something unique, extraordinary. The Bible may be mistaken about its own claim to be historically accurate, but even if it is, it still is fundamentally correct when it sets itself apart from all other Homeric-like stories, in reference to the truth, when it accuses them of lying. As long as one believes that there is, in principle, a fundamental difference between reality and fiction, between that which truly is and that which is only an imitation, a counterfeit, one must also believe in the uniqueness of the Bible, at least within the context of the origins of Western culture. The origin of the belief in such a fundamental difference, the difference that allows Auerbach himself to distinguish clearly between the two styles, is to be found in the "passionate" interest of the biblical narrative in the truth of historical reality. We learned it first from the Bible. Outside the biblical world, one would have to wait for Plato to find a similar interest in the truth, although not exactly in the truth of history.

We must also point out that the Bible, as we can see in the words of the Psalmist, does not claim to know all the truth, everything there is to know. Quite the contrary: he asks God for illumination, he wants to know the truth, he pleads for knowledge. It is not his truth, it is God's truth, and he trusts God. It is because he has faith in God that he is "passionately" interested in the truth. His is a trusted God who does not lie, and keeps his promises. This God is the necessary mediator between the Psalmist and the reality, the truth, of the world out there. And that changes everything before his eyes. What he rejects is not other claims to the truth, but, as we will see in a moment, the manner of "those who speak lies," "mockers," "illusionists," "double-minded men," who are not interested in the truth, because they do not love and follow God's commandments. The sacred character of the world is nothing to be afraid of, only if God, the name of the sacred itself, is with you. Which implies that if this were not so, if God's guaranty were not there to protect you, there would be no enduring, safe way to avoid disaster, to prevent the sacred world out there from turning against you. It is either God's way or you would have to find yourself a way of cheating disaster itself, of luring it, ensnaring it, enchanting it out of your way—or perhaps appeasing it, baiting it with all kinds of substitute victims so that it may spare you.

In other words, the choice was never between what the Bible claims to be the truth, and other such claims, but between the Bible's manner of relating to and representing the truth, and Homer's manner. Auerbach's mistake was to believe that Homer's way of representing reality consisted basically in ignoring it and freely choosing to create a make-believe reality of his own. The critic saw reality and the truth with modern eyes; that is to say, as desacralized concepts that exist by themselves in complete independence from sacred connotations or interferences. He could only see the sacred as a conceptual addition to reality and truth, but basically extraneous to them. He never wonders about the long road traveled by the concept of truth from biblical to modern times, and the extent to which the end result, our modern desacralized understanding of the truth, is indebted (paradoxically, perhaps, in the eyes of some) to the biblical trust and faith in the sacred reality and truth of the world out there. Without that original trust, without the biblical God's promise of support, our modern desacralized and scientific knowledge of the world would not have been possible.[19] The question of truth was an ontological and sacred question before it could ever become an epistemological one. Our confidence before the world would have never come about as a result of Homer's manner of dealing with reality and truth. It took the biblical liberation of the truth and of the world at large from all Homeric types of enchantments due to fear, to make it possible to be where we are today. It is, therefore, profoundly ironic for Auerbach to think of the "tyrannical" view of the truth in the Bible, while offering us the reading of a quasi-modern Homer, who flippantly ignores the truth to give us some "harmless" entertainment.

However, to judge by the testimony of the Bible itself, the exemplary faith of Abraham, of the people of Israel, in the truth was not easy. The temptation was always there to fall back into what we may now call in general the Homeric way, which appears to have been the easier way, in a sense, the "natural" way, after the Fall, after the original sacrificial crisis—or, if we may use the computer language of today, the "default" way of looking for protection against the sacred character of that which is *truly* out there. In other words, it was either the hard Jewish way or the tempting easy way of the Homeric style. What is difficult to imagine in these circumstances is that third possibility contemplated in a purely hypothetical manner by Auerbach in the person of a rationalistic "political liar," who would only pretend to believe in the truth of the Bible for political gain. I do not think this type of modern liar was possible in that context. It would imply the possibility of facing up to the unavoidably sacred character of the reality out there without any sacred protection whatsoever, either the hard one or the easy one. That does not seem possible. If you did not follow the biblical way, you were inevitably following the Homeric way, the pagan way, in any of its multiple varieties. There was no other ground to stand on, no modern agnosticism, no way to escape the sacred face of reality.

There can be no doubt that Abraham's faith was a very hard one to keep. In a sense, that is the whole point of the story of Abraham's sacrifice of Isaac—the paradigmatic story that, at least to modern eyes,[20] confers on Abraham the title of Father of the Faith. It is there that his faith is being sorely tested, or, to put it in the language of the King James version, "tempted." It is the biblical story par excellence in the Old Testament, revealing in a dramatic way the foundation upon which all the other biblical stories rest, since everything stands on Abraham's unshakable faith in God, even when God appears to contradict Himself, to go back on His promise. Auerbach could not have chosen a more radically anti-Odyssean, anti-Homeric story. Abraham's faith is inconceivable, utterly impossible, in the Homeric world. Such a faith would be either incomprehensible or terrifying, or both.

It is also the story that answers Auerbach's question about the biblical narrator's need to believe in the truth of what it narrates. Just as Odysseus's style and story explain the reason for the Homeric "lie," the creation of an enchanting world of make-believe, so does the story of Abraham's sacrifice explain the ultimate reason for the narrator to believe in the historical truth of what he narrates. He believes in the truth of the story because he believes in the same God in which Abraham believed. The faith of Abraham is not only the faith of Abraham, it is also the faith of the biblical narrator. He not only narrates the story of Abraham, he has faith in it. In other words, the story of Abraham, which he narrates, explains why he has faith in the historical truth of the story of Abraham. It is his story too, the story of his faith. He believes in its historical reality for exactly the same reason that Abraham believed and acted the way he did. They both believe in the truth because they both believe in a God who is the God of the truth, the God who sustains the truth of the world out there, the mediator between them and that which is truly there. They cannot separate faith in God and God's promise, on the one hand, and faith in the historical truth, on the other. The biblical God is hidden, as Auerbach noticed, but he is still the God of the world out there. In this regard it is important to understand that God's promise to Abraham does not involve something like the Christian Kingdom of Heaven. The object of the promise is fully within the realm of human history. It concerns

Abraham's earthly existence and that of his entire progeny to the end of time. It is a promise about the history of humanity.

It is worth noticing, too, that this kind of personal identification of the biblical narrator with the story that he narrates and its protagonist cannot occur in the case of Homer, by definition. Odysseus's story does indeed explain the reason for the Homeric "lie": Homer imitates Odysseus, but precisely because of that there can be no bond of faith between them. You may admire a liar, you may imitate him, but you would be foolish to put your faith in him. And Homer is too good for that. He knows exactly what he is doing. In fact, how could anybody have faith in Odysseus? He is the original embodiment of the warning never to let your guard down against deceiving appearances. Nonetheless, it seems that humanity has always found it easier to follow Odysseus's warning than the faithful example of Abraham.

Maybe that is why God put Abraham to the test with a terrible temptation. He orders Abraham to do something, to offer Isaac as "a holocaust," which is not only extremely painful, but something that would make it humanly, logically impossible for the promise to be fulfilled. Will he waver in his faith? Will he doubt? Will he become bitter, anxious? Will he remind God of what He told him? For Abraham is quite capable of asking questions of God. He has done it before. At the very least, will his hand tremble, will he close his eyes, as he raises the sacrificial knife over Isaac, his only son, "whom he loves," given to him and Sarah in their old age by God himself? Does he remember at this awful moment how he first and then Sarah laughed, seeing that they were so old, when they heard from God that they would have a son? The biblical narrator, the Elohist, is as silent about Abraham's "realistic" thoughts and feelings as Abraham himself is, even though those, or any other such feelings and thoughts, must be assumed. For if they are not assumed, the test, qua test, would lose its meaning. It had to be something extremely painful, the sort of thing that, if properly expressed and detailed, would have made for an inexhaustible source of poetic delight. One can only think of what the Greeks did with Agamemnon's sacrifice of his daughter Iphigenia. But none of that draws the attention of the biblical narrator. All poetic delight, all seductive "lures," all "enchantment" would divert him from his task. There is only one important question at that horrendous moment, before which everything else pales and disappears: Will Abraham keep his faith? Will he still believe that God will keep His promise? And the answer is that obviously he does. Against all human and logical evidence, he keeps his faith. For he shows not the slightest hesitation. He will obey in silence, without addressing a single word to God, and without ever doubting. The only words that break the silence are Isaac's words, "My father . . . where is the lamb for a burnt offering?," and the father's reply, "God will provide Himself the lamb for a burnt offering, my son." Nothing else, just his faith. No wonder that Auerbach felt that the story is "fraught with background."

There is still another aspect of the test, which makes it even more terrible. The idea of sacrificing your son to a god, reference to which appears on numerous occasions in the Bible, is always presented as an abomination, strictly forbidden by the God of Israel:

> They built the high places of Baal in the Valley of the son of Hinnom to offer up their sons and daughters to Molech, though I did not command them, nor did it enter into my mind, that they should do this abomination, to cause Judah to sin. (Jeremiah 32:35)

The passage refers to the sacrificial burning alive of children in the cult of Baal or Moloch, the gods that even Abraham's ancestors may have worshiped. Detestable and horrible though such things were, they were by no means unheard of. In other words, God is testing or tempting Abraham with something that was specifically associated with idol worship—the kind of temptation felt by the chosen people throughout their biblical history. For time and again, the people of Israel lapse into idolatry. They want to do what all the other people around them are doing—people without a covenant, with no faith of their own, because no god had promised them anything. It was obviously difficult to swim against the current, so to speak. The prophets cry out constantly against these breaches of faith, these idolatrous lapses, mentioning in particular, repeatedly, the cult of Baal. Was God laying a trap for Abraham? In other words, it would have been perfectly understandable if Abraham had wondered whether the God who ordered him to sacrifice Isaac was in fact his God, the God of the promise. Could it have been a diabolical ploy, Baal in disguise? Such wondering, however, though understandable, would not have been in keeping with his faith. He would have failed the test miserably if he had reasoned with himself along such lines as these: "The true God could not possibly demand such an evil thing from me. He is not that kind of God." Obviously he did not reason that way. He could not. He knew it was his God. Such knowledge was intrinsic to the test itself. He could not escape it. And such thoughts would have been an escape. He did not have that option. But that made the test all the more difficult, doubly difficult. Because the horror was not only in the act itself, the killing of Isaac, but also in the fact that it was his God, in whose righteousness and justice he had placed his entire confidence, who asked him to do it. Even if he was ready to sacrifice the son he loved, could he still see God in the same way he had always seen Him? In principle, from a psychological point of view, he could obey God's command and still inwardly lose his faith in Him; perform the sacrifice and profoundly regret it at the same time. Which, of course, would have altered his relationship with God. Obviously that did not happen either.

We must ask, therefore, how did Abraham see God? That is to say, what does the biblical story imply about the way God appeared in the eyes of Abraham's unshakable faith? It is not enough to say that his God is the one who keeps his promise, who never lies. He is even more than totally truthful and trustworthy; indeed He is greater than truth itself, because He is the foundation on which truth stands, the one who gives value and meaning to the truth—the truth of truth, as it were. Truth does not extend beyond Him. In other words, He is not truthful and reliable because He is willing to adhere to some universal standard of veracity or morality, the rationality of which exists independently of Him, and according to which Abraham could have judged Him. On the contrary, His trustworthiness extends past human comprehension. In the final analysis, Abraham's trust in Him cannot be dependent on any rational explanation. It is a "leap of faith," as Kierkegaard would call it—not into the irrational, but into the unknown, fully trusting that you will land on solid ground, even when all the logical evidence appears to point to the contrary. Because God's word is the only thing on which you can completely rely. And since He created the world and everything in it, you can also trust in the ultimate truth of the world out there. History and the world are real and truthful, beyond all transient circumstances, because God is there supporting them.

But this is perhaps the point at which we should bring back for a moment one of those "rationalistic interpreters" to which Auerbach was referring. He or she will, of course, believe that the biblical story of Abraham's sacrifice never actually happened. It was all made up somehow. But by whom?

Perhaps by an inspired liar like Odysseus or Homer, one of those "who know how to say many false things that were like true sayings." But as soon as we assume that, we begin to notice some surprising features. Perhaps the most obvious one is an appalling dearth of poetic details, as Auerbach was the first to notice. But this also means that the supposedly inspired liar has made no effort whatsoever to make the story credible, which is the basic requirement, the sine qua non, of the art of lying. If a lie is not verisimilar, truth-like, it will not work. Not only did he not make any effort to make the lie credible, he seemed to be working precisely in the opposite direction, by simplifying the plot so much that even the very few empirical details given, like the brief exchange between father and son, do not seem to be essential to the story. The story is practically reduced to its bare bones. Which means it has no entertainment value or purpose. And, in essence—the "rationalistic interpreter" must admit—the narrating liar wants us to believe that a man named Abraham became so absolutely convinced of the reality of an imaginary all-powerful god who had promised him the world, so to speak, that he was willing to sacrifice everything on the altar of such a god, to the point where he actually was on the verge of sacrificing his only son. Fortunately for the son—so the incredible story goes—something happened at the last moment (the man thought he heard the voice of God), and the son was spared.

Clearly it would take an enormous amount of detailing and lying artistry to turn that kind of saying into something that looks "like true sayings," assuming that it could be done at all. And the point is that the narrator not only did not even try, but by reducing the story to its bare bones seemed to be arguing or implying that we should believe it because the man named Abraham, the protagonist of the story that he, the narrating liar, has invented, was absolutely convinced that it was all true. Let me repeat: it looks like the assumed inventor of the story of Abraham, who aims not at entertainment, but at convincing us that the story is true, argues or implies that we should be so convinced because the protagonist he has invented for his story says so (whether there really was a man named Abraham is irrelevant here). A rather interesting circularity, as our "rationalistic interpreter" must also admit.

In other words, if this whole story is a deliberate lie, the liar was a fool who did not know what he was doing. He was indeed an incredibly bad liar, nothing at all like Homer or Odysseus. Or did he actually think that his Jewish audience could swallow anything no matter how badly done? If he did, he was not only a bad liar, he was also stupid. And, if I may borrow Cervantes's condemnation of an author who had committed a similar type of foolishness, "he deserves to be sent to the galleys for the rest of his life."[21]

The mention of Cervantes at this moment is deliberate, of course. If the story of Abraham's sacrifice, the story that, above all others, confers on Abraham the title Father of the Faith, is all made up; if the faith portrayed there is illusory; if the God that Abraham trusts does not exist, or never had any direct communication with him in any form, linguistic or otherwise, then the man Abraham is truly a madman, a complete fool pathologically obsessed with an illusion so powerful that it obliterates his sense of reality and makes him see and hear things that are not really there. If the bad and foolish liar, the inventor of the story, had really understood what he was doing, that is in truth the story he should have told, the story of Abraham the fool—that is to say, the story of Don Quixote by another name. That would have made sense; that would have been believable in the eyes of our "rationalistic interpreter," even if it never really happened. In other words, if the God who put Abraham to the test is no less legendary than Zeus, or for that matter, Amadís of Gaul, "the sun of Knight Errantry," the first and foremost, then there is no fundamental difference between Don Quixote and Abraham. Psychologically speaking, it is the same kind of madness. Except that it appears to be much deeper and thorough in the case of Abraham. After all, Don Quixote was only mad "in patches" (*un loco entreverado*). But there are no patches, no cracks, in Abraham's maddening "illusion." His "illusory" God demands total, absolute allegiance. Madness for madness, Abraham is by far the madder of the two. On the other hand, if Abraham is not mad, and the biblical narrator is not a fool who does not know what he is doing, then we are not dealing with an invented story, with a lie made to look like true sayings. From which we may deduce in perfectly good logic that the story can be essentially true beyond the few empirical details given, which may or may not be considered necessary for a full understanding of its message. But even if one does not believe in the historical objectivity of the story of Abraham's sacrifice, one cannot treat it as a fictional story. It cannot be turned into a piece of Homeric make-believe. Furthermore, as soon as we place it in an ambiguous context where the difference between truth and fiction becomes blurred, the biblical story of Abraham's faith stops making sense. Abraham's faith requires not only a true God, but a true world out there—a world the reality of which is as solid and unassailable as God Himself, and as sacred, of course.

In other words, if Abraham's faith is not illusory, if we accept his story as it appears in the Bible, then such a story is the anti-quixotic story par excellence, the very antidote to Don Quixote's madness, because it is the story that cannot be fictionalized without turning it into its very opposite—without, in fact, destroying it. Correspondingly, one may define the story of Don Quixote's madness as the story of the destruction, of the falsifying, of the faith of Abraham; or rather, of the turning of the faith of Abraham into its counterfeit, a psychologically destructive counterfeit.

It all depends on whether the mediator between the man and the world out there is real or a piece of invented fiction. We know why Don Quixote went mad, why he got into his head the insane idea that "shining," invincible Amadís of Gaul, "the sun of knight errantry," the greatest knight ever recorded, was real, and he, Don Quixote, had to follow in his footsteps. The reason was that the poor Manchegan hidalgo had spent years doing nothing but reading fascinating novels about knights errant. That is to say, he had been seduced, lured, enchanted, by all those lies. As a result, Amadís of Gaul became like a god in his eyes. He saw what Amadís saw, according to those books of chivalry. Amadís did not see windmills, but giants; not ordinary road inns, but enchanted castles. And Don Quixote put his faith in Amadís. Fiction bred fiction.

But there is no lure, no snare, no enchanting web in the case of Abraham. The mediator between him and the world out there is God Himself, who, by definition, cannot seduce Abraham away from the truth of anything, because He is the creator of everything that is truly out there. Abraham sees everything that he can possibly see as a human being through the eyes of God, so to speak. God is, therefore, the source and the object of his unimaginable faith. The enormity of his faith, its "patchless" solidity, is a reflection of the power of God. Compared with it the strength of Don Quixote's faith in Amadís, full of "patches," is like nothing. Which means that when we speak of Abraham's madness in strictly human, psychological terms, we fall short. Abraham's faith is actually beyond madness. And if Don Quixote's madness could destroy him, we can well imagine what Abraham's faith could do to him, to any man, if it turned out to be illusory, if it turned out that God is not what Abraham thinks. Therefore, it is God who brings Abraham to the edge of the abyss, and also God who saves him from it. It is God who tests or "tempts" Abraham, and who gives him the strength to withstand the test. But who could invent such a story? Who could invent Abraham's faith? There lies a mystery for which we have no explanation that could even remotely satisfy our "rationalistic interpreter."

We must emphasize the mediating role or function that God has in the story of Abraham's faith. To repeat, He mediates between Abraham and the reality of the world out there. God may love his servant Abraham or his people, Israel, but I think that in the eyes of Abraham, He is first and foremost the creator of the world. It is His world, even though He is not part of it. He owns it, and everything in it. Because He is true, He is also the guarantor of the truth of the reality out there. I do not think that Abraham's faith is any sort of mystical union with the divinity. It is in this sense a very realistic, even materialistic type of faith, fundamentally oriented towards the reality of history and the vicissitudes of human society.

The alternative to the God of Abraham and to his faith is the world as seen and confronted by the Homeric singer. Odysseus is the representative and the voice of such a world, a profoundly ambivalent and ambiguous world. Nothing at all like the solid one of Abraham's faith. The Homeric singer is a creature of that world. He does not make it up. He responds to the ambivalence and the ambiguity in which he lives. Everything he does to make up his poetic world, to imagine "many false things as though they were true," is suggested to him by the nature of the world out there. It would be absurd, and painfully unsettling, to have faith in such a world. The only sensible and urgent thing to do is to build some protection around oneself: a poetic protection made of the same ambiguous material as offered by the world out there. The Homeric singer had no choice in the matter. He had no place to hide from an ambiguity that was as sacred to him as God's world was to the biblical narrator. It was the unavoidable sacred itself that appeared to him as deeply ambivalent and ambiguous, both a remedy and a terrifying threat—a cure if he managed to keep it at bay, and a lethal disease if it came too close. As we have already indicated, Homer's "make-believe" is very serious business, much more than mere entertainment. Hence the difference also with Cervantes's *Don Quixote*. The novelistic fiction in Don Quixote's mind is in no way related to the reality of the world out there, the world in which Cervantes (and the Manchegan hidalgo Alonso Quijano) lived. Cervantes's real world had been molded by, and was heir to, Abraham's faith. It was then that Homeric make-believe stopped being serious business and truly became pure entertainment, and to believe otherwise, as Don Quixote did, was sheer madness.

Abraham's faith and the mythical world of Homer are incompatible, but both are, each in its own way, a modus vivendi, a way of truly living in a world that was unavoidably sacred, and finding a safe way to do it.

Here are the words of the Psalmist again:

> *I hate double-minded men,*
> *But I love your law.*
> *You are my hiding place and my shield;*
> *I hope in your word.*
> *Depart from me, you evildoers,*
> *That I may keep the commandments of my God.*
> . . .
> *I hate and abhor falsehood [or "delusion"],*
> *but I love your law.* (Psalm 119:113–115, 163)

Let me paraphrase: "I hate double-minded men, Lord, you are my hiding place, not them, I trust your word, not their word. Get away from me, you double-minded evildoers . . . because I hate your falsehood, your delusion." The new Latin version of the Vulgate calls them *duplices corde*, "duplicitous at heart"—that is to say, ambivalent, ambiguous providers of delusion, of falsehood.[22] The Psalmist is probably concerned about "double-minded men" who thought they could worship Yahweh and still cling to the old sacred ways of Baal, for example.[23] We do not really know. But whoever it was that the Psalmist had in mind, it seems to me that the description fits the Homeric singer perfectly. However, what I would like to point out at this moment it is not so much the accusation of duplicity, ambivalence, or falsehood, but the fact that the Psalmist is clearly implying that the work of the "double-minded" men is meant to be a "hiding place," a "shield," which he rejects because he has a better one: the Lord Himself is his hiding place and his shield. In other words, he does not believe in the protection value of fictional constructs. He does not believe that one can find true protection behind the foolish words of double-minded men and their ambiguous lies.

But indirectly he confirms what we are trying to say: that the Homeric make-believe, the hiding of the truth, is a way of hiding from the truth in fear, a way to protect oneself, a refuge.

This way of looking at the lies of "double-minded" men as a refuge finds, in my view, a stunning confirmation in the words of the prophet Isaiah, as he addresses the "scoffers" in Jerusalem (Vulgate's *viri illusores*, i.e., jokers, illusionists), or the "mockers," or, in still other versions, those "who make fun of the truth," in a rather sarcastic, though extremely penetrating, way. The prophet mocks the mockers:

> *Therefore hear the word of the Lord, you scoffers,*
> *Who rule this people in Jerusalem!*
> *Because you have said, "We have made a covenant with death,*
> *And with Sheol we have an agreement;*
> *When the overwhelming scourge passes through*
> *It will not come to us;*
> *For we have made lies our refuge,*
> *And in falsehood we have taken shelter";*
> *Therefore thus says the Lord God,*
> *"Behold, I am laying in Zion for a foundation*
> *A stone, a tested stone,*
> *A precious cornerstone, of a sure foundation:*
> *'He who believes will not be in haste.'*
> *And I will make justice the line,*
> *And righteousness the plummet;*
> *And hail will sweep away the refuge of lies,*
> *And waters will overwhelm the shelter."*
> *Then your covenant with death will be annulled,*
> *and your agreement with Sheol will not stand;*
> *when the overwhelming scourge passes through*
> *you will be beaten down by it.*
>
> . . . .
>
> *and it will be sheer terror to understand the message.*
>
> . . . .
>
> *For the Lord will rise up . . . to do his deed—strange is his deed!*
> *And to work his work—alien is his work!* (Isaiah 28:14–19)

It is a difficult passage, which offers nonetheless a glimpse of unfathomable depth. Let us paraphrase again. This is essentially what the prophet is saying explicitly, or clearly implying, as he addresses the "scoffers" of the truth: We, the faithful people of Abraham, have a covenant with God. This is where we take refuge against death and destruction; this is our protection against the "overwhelming scourge." But you do not have, or have abandoned, such a protection. Instead, you scoffers, jokers, illusionists do indeed live under an illusion. You say you have made a pact with death and hell, in other words, with the scourge itself, for that is what the scourge brings along, what the scourge is made of. But what you have really done is to fabricate a hiding place with lies and simulations. That is what you call a pact, a lie that, like all lies, you hope will succeed in deceiving your overwhelming enemy. In other words, you hope your enemy will pass by without seeing through your lie, without seeing you inside your lie. You think you can deceive death and hell, the "overwhelming scourge." But listen, the Lord has already seen through your lies, and is, therefore, building up a true shelter against such an enemy, on an enduring foundation, not on lies, for those who believe, who will not have to run away in panic ("as you do" is the obvious implication), for they will have no fear. And the truth of this shelter, built with justice and righteousness, will expose the lies of your hiding place for what they really are, thereby sweeping away your protection, for you were only protected by deceiving appearances, which will lose their protection value as soon as the deception is brought out into the open. Therefore, in plain sight of the true shelter, your covenant with death will be annulled and your agreement with Hell will not stand any longer. Every time the overwhelming scourge passes through, it will crush you. And when you understand what has happened, why your lies can no longer protect you, it will be sheer terror. For the Lord is rising up and doing something strange indeed, something unheard of.

Biblical exegetes have frequently interpreted this passage, and, in particular, the "overwhelming scourge," as referring to the Assyrian invasion of the Northern Kingdom as well as of Judah. In other words, here too, as in other passages in which Isaiah is perfectly explicit about it, God is using the Assyrians, or the Egyptians, as an instrument of his punishment of Israel. This may be part of the historical context that brings about the prophecy. But it seems to me that the prophecy itself goes far beyond historical particularities. The "overwhelming scourge" in this passage is much more than a literary metaphor for Assyrian power. If "death" and "hell" in this context simply equal "Assyrian power," how does one lie to the Assyrians in order to be protected from their "overwhelming scourge"? And why would the Assyrians need the help of the Lord to build a true shelter against death and destruction in order to see through the deceiving nature of the "refuge of lies"? Even if the prophet is directly warning those people who were contemplating alliances with Assyria or Egypt, what he sees them doing has a universal dimension.[24] In a way that transcends the historical circumstances of whatever pacts they were contemplating, the prophet sees them as operating under an illusion; they are jokers, they do not really know what they are doing, they are like the "drunkards of Ephrain," they could not care less about the truth. But their illusion is a universal one.[25]

The prophet, of course, speaks already from the perspective of the refuge that the Lord is building on an everlasting foundation. It is from that perspective that he sees the scoffers, the illusionists making a pact with violence, with death, in order to protect themselves from violence. Or, to use words closer to those of Christ in the Gospel, making a pact with Satan to protect themselves from Satan. After all, Christians have always believed that Christ is precisely the "tested," the "precious cornerstone" anticipated in the prophecy, the stone that will turn out to be also the one "that the builders rejected" (Psalm 118:22). But what are they offering to Satan, to the onslaught of violence, in exchange for protection? The prophet tells us that they offer a lie, for that is their refuge, that is what they are hiding behind, a falsehood—which seems rather appropriate in a satanic context, Satan being the father of lies. They offer, therefore, a false appearance to the onslaught of violence, in the hope of diverting the terrible violence away from themselves. In other words, they hope to deceive that with which they are making a pact, for they are not offering anything real, but something made up, a substitute, once again in the hope that the onslaught will take it and spare them, who are hiding behind the lie. But today we know about such a substitute, or decoy, or false front, which human society, the *civitas terrena*, has offered from the beginning to the god of violence. It is called a sacrificial victim. The only pact that human beings have ever made with "overwhelming violence" in order to be spared is the sacrificial pact.

The prophet is talking, therefore, about what the prophets of Israel have always talked about: idolatrous sacrifice, into which the chosen people lapsed time and time again. But this time Isaiah exposes the true nature of the idol. He does not waste any time telling his people, as we see in so many other prophecies, that those figures made of wood or metal are lifeless and cannot be gods. What they are really worshiping beyond the wood and the metal is violence itself, overwhelming violence. Worshiping the lifeless idol is a way of averting the violence behind it. And all idols require substitute victims, because they are the external sign—the voice, as it were—of overwhelming violence. The lie, the deception, is the lifeless idol itself as well as the victim that goes with it. What I think is new in this prophetic passage is the view of the internal logic of the sacrificial process itself as a form of deception, a "refuge of lies." And this is truly amazing.

First of all, Yahweh Himself appears as a sacrificial god in the Old Testament. The more clearly so, the further back we go in Jewish history as preserved in the different books of the Bible, regardless of when each of these books was composed or by whom. He demands sacrifices on numerous occasions. The "altar of the holocaust" was a central feature in the temple of Jerusalem. But in Isaiah we begin to see a different conception of God. The "Lord God" of Isaiah is not just the jealous and violent God of Joshua, for example, who does not want His people to sacrifice to any other god but Him. He is no longer interested in sacrifices at all. They are "vain offerings" to Him:

> 11 *"What to me is the multitude of your sacrifices?*
> *says the LORD;*
> *I have had enough of burnt offerings of rams*
> *and the fat of well-fed beasts;*
> *I do not delight in the blood of bulls,*
> *or of lambs, or of goats.*
> 12 *"When you come to appear before me,*
> *who has required of you*
> *this trampling of my courts?*
> 13 *Bring no more vain offerings;*
> *incense is an abomination to me.*
> *New moon and Sabbath and the calling of convocations—*
> *I cannot endure iniquity and solemn assembly.*
> 14 *Your new moons and your appointed feasts*
> *my soul hates;*

they have become a burden to me;
I am weary of bearing them.
15 *When you spread out your hands,*
I will hide my eyes from you;
even though you make many prayers,
I will not listen;
your hands are full of blood.
16 *Wash yourselves; make yourselves clean;*
remove the evil of your deeds from before my eyes;
cease to do evil,
17 *learn to do good;*
seek justice,
correct oppression;
bring justice to the fatherless,
plead the widow's cause. (Isaiah 1:11–17)

Something fundamental has happened here to the biblical concept of God. This new vision of a God who is no longer interested in ritual sacrifices, and, therefore, no longer interested in all those sacred cultural differences that separate one people from another, must also be the vision of a God who looks beyond "the tribes of Jacob." A God with a universal mission of salvation:

And now the LORD says,
he who formed me from the womb to be his servant,
to bring Jacob back to him;
and that Israel might be gathered to him—
for I am honored in the eyes of the LORD,
and my God has become my strength—
6 *he says: "It is too light a thing that you should be my servant*
to raise up the tribes of Jacob
and to bring back the preserved of Israel;
I will make you as a light for the nations,
that my salvation may reach to the end of the earth." (Isaiah 49:5–6)

In this new conception of God, of which we get clear indications in Isaiah, God cannot ultimately be the God of the "overwhelming scourge," in other words, the God of vengeance. For it seems that, at least here, He is not fighting violence with violence. The new shelter He is building, based on justice and righteousness, is a shelter inside which fear of the "overwhelming scourge" will simply disappear for those who believe. It does not look like a God who overwhelms the "overwhelming scourge," but rather like a God who disarms the scourge, who turns it into something no longer capable of frightening the faithful into worshiping submission. In other words, I think what this new conception of God does is to undermine the sacralization of violence, and, as a result, the pact with death and hell based on lies. The "overwhelming scourge" is not God, even though it will, de facto, become an instrument of God for those who do not believe in the true shelter, for those who place their trust in a "refuge of lies"—which is another way of saying, for those who already have turned the "overwhelming scourge" into a god, for those who have sacralized human violence.

None of this implies that the "overwhelming scourge" will disappear as a physical threat. Clearly God could produce an "overwhelming scourge," any kind of disaster, anytime against those who deserve it. He may even test the faithful with calamity. Hence the words of the Psalmist, "The Lord has chastened me sorely, / but he has not given me over to death" (Psalm 118:18). That is to say, the Lord saves me from the satanic power of death, not necessarily from death as a physical phenomenon. In Christianity, this process becomes radicalized. Christ submits willingly to the "overwhelming scourge" in order to break its sacred power, its sacred stranglehold on humanity. Christ's radical revelation is that of the nonviolent God. He is not God of the dead but of the living; the power of death is no longer sacred.

The real novelty in Isaiah, it seems to me, is the revelation and denunciation of idolatry as a pact with death, which is a form of fiction. Or, to put it in terms more closely related to the theme of this essay, the denunciation of fiction as a sacred shield or shelter against overpowering violence. But we must be careful with our own use of the word "fiction" in this context. The prophet is not saying exactly that the illusion, the lie as a refuge, is not going to work simply because it is a lie, an illusion. It is not going to work *because* the Lord will do something that will make it fail ("*Because* you have said . . . *Therefore* thus says the Lord God . . ."). And what the Lord is going to do is to build a true refuge on "a sure foundation," by means of "justice and righteousness." It is this true refuge that will put an end to "the refuge of lies": "Then your covenant with death will be annulled." Clearly it is the new refuge, based on truth, that will reveal the old one as a lie, as something baseless that will be swept away, when the "overwhelming scourge passes through." As I said before, when the prophet talks about the "refuge of lies," he is already talking from the perspective of the new and truthful refuge.

But it is going to take nothing less than the decisive action of the Lord God to expose the "refuge of lies" for what it really is. Which is, by implication, an acknowledgment of the power of attraction of such a refuge or hiding place. Until the decisive action of the Lord takes place, the sacrificial lie will continue to attract in its double dimension: as a sacrificial mask *stricto sensu*, and as the poetic mask that "lures" and "snares" with lies that "look like true sayings," for the Homeric lie is also a sacrificial lie. These are only two ways of talking about the same thing, two ways of worshiping, sacralizing, human violence—or to be more precise, the hellish, the enslaving, spirit of human violence.

Why the sacrificial lie was such an explicit and constant temptation to the people of the covenant is a topic well deserving of extensive meditation, which goes beyond the limits of our study. But it is important to take notice of it. As we said before, Abraham's way was the hard way; Homer's was the easy, and in a sense, the natural way after the Fall. In the face of overwhelming danger, it seems easier, more animal-like, more instinctive, to play dead, to disguise oneself, to hide. Abraham's faith and trust in God is definitely not the most immediate and natural reaction, even though it may eventually turn out to be the only lasting one, the one that makes the threat itself disappear as a threat to the spirit; that is to say, as a source of fear and panic.

The unreflective, almost instinctive sentiment that pagan rituals, including all sorts of fiction-making activities, were fundamentally defensive in nature, a way to protect oneself from danger, was something noticed by Saint Augustine with no small puzzlement. He devotes a large portion of *The City of God* to answer the charge that the fall of the city of Rome to the Goths of Alaric in 410 A.D., and in general the gradual demise of the Roman empire, was due to the disappearance of the old gods from the city, because of the rapidly expanding faith of the Christians. The charge was that the abandonment of the old gods left the city defenseless, an easy target for all kinds of disasters. The saint sounds more than a little puzzled by the charge: does that mean that Rome was immune from disaster before Christianity arrived? He surveys the history of Rome so full of horrendous happenings since its very foundation, in particular its incredibly bloody civil wars. Why—he asks—do they not blame their gods for those calamities? They did not do a good job of protecting the city. And if they never blamed their gods, why do they now blame Christ? His outrage becomes acute when he considers what actually happened during the sack of Rome by the Goths. The pillage and carnage must have been severe, but many people, Christians and pagans, took refuge in Christian temples and were saved, because actually the Goths of Alaric, who were Arians, respected those temples—probably the only thing they respected. And still, to the saint's amazement, those same pagans who were saved in those temples continued to say that the whole thing happened because the gods had been abandoned! Did the Trojan gods, who were the same as the Greek gods, protect their worshipers when they were brutally massacred by the Greeks inside their temples, right at the very foot of their altars?

I think that behind the understandable ardor of the Christian apologist lies a very serious and penetrating question. Why could those ungrateful pagans not see Christ as a line of defense against disaster, while on the other hand, they would continue to see their gods and rituals in no other way but as such a defense, in spite of all the evidence testifying to their failure? The answer, I think, is in the text of Isaiah, in the "covenant with death" that idolaters believe will protect them from the "overwhelming scourge"; that is to say, from ultimate violence, and by extension, from any kind of violent onslaught.

As we have just said, the idolater sacralizes the very violence from which he wants to find protection; he turns it into a god, conferring on it some sort of satanic transcendence. Without this worshiping of the very violence that threatens him, the pagan feels vulnerable, defenseless. This is why he turns every danger, every uncertainty, every problematic transition, into a god or a devil. He sees the face of the sacred lurking behind every possible threat, and he immediately makes a pact with it, prays to be protected from the danger by the danger itself.[26] The Greeks, for example, "spoke of famine and pestilence as 'gods.'"[27] The more real and greater the danger, the more of an urgent need to kneel before it as a protection. How could such a worshiper ever see Christ as a protection against the "overwhelming scourge"? And from his perspective he is right, because indeed Christ has nothing to do with it. Worse than that from a pagan perspective, Christ desacralizes the violent onslaught, and asks the faithful to see it as human violence pure and simple, which is the truth. But that is not going to stop the onslaught at the moment, and the Christian must be ready to die. A true Christian, a true follower of Christ in a world that sacralizes violence, is inherently a martyr, and as such, a witness to the truth. Of course, if everybody adopts such an attitude, nobody has to die. And the true Christian constantly looks forward to such a possibility. But the pagan is not looking forward to tomorrow, he is only concerned with the violent onslaught today. This is why, again from a pagan perspective, there is logic and truth in the pagan feeling of vulnerability in the face of violence, if all he has for protection is Christ.

On the other hand, how can the pagan ever rise in protest against his gods for not protecting him against violence, when in the very act of worshiping them, he is locating in them the source of the violence while pleading with them not to strike? How can you blame your gods for anything, when at the same time you are also trying to appease them, or to deceive them, by covering yourself with a mask?

This pagan rush to turn every danger, every calamity, into a greater or lesser god is obviously much more than a bit of homeopathic magic.[28] Behind this endless multitude of gods big and small lies the "covenant with death" of which the prophet spoke, the satanic worship of the "overwhelming scourge," Satan against Satan. A procedure that in Girardian terms is called the "victimage mechanism," the hypermimetic violent crisis that produces the victim that will save everybody, at least temporarily.

It is also important to realize at this point that the victimage mechanism and its resulting "covenant with death" or idol worshiping worked relatively well. It allowed a fallen and deceived humanity to survive. Cities were founded and civilization flourished. Those were, and are, clear benefits. In other words, the "overwhelming scourge" was contained, in the two senses of the word: it was brought in as a god, and thus sacralized; it was also kept within bounds, managed, made into all kinds of beneficial institutions. The hellish Erynies turning into gracious Eumenides could be the universal symbol of this civilization-producing transformation. Even though ultimately based on lies and deception, the *civitas terrena* is not a fiction. Nor is the "overwhelming scourge"—that is to say, hypermimetic, open-ended human violence—a fiction either. What is a fiction is the sacralizing of it. In this regard, pagan sacralization equals fictionalization, and vice versa.

We must insist on this. The fact that Christianity has revealed that the "overwhelming scourge" is not a god, and has given hope to humanity that violence will not have the last word on the final destiny of the human race, does not mean that fear of open-ended, apocalyptic violence is unjustified. Quite the contrary, as Girard has repeatedly pointed out: the desacralization of violence, the relentless historical erosion of the victimage mechanism, accelerates the violence and spreads it in ever-widening circles as it deprives humanity of its immemorial defense mechanism. When no victim is any longer capable of generating unanimity around its expulsion or elimination, as is the case today, the result has not been a cessation of the sacrificial mentality, but the very opposite: a frantic search for victims all over. As Christ said, "I have not come to bring peace, but a sword" (Matthew 10:34).

Today in the West—that is to say, in that part of the world most directly influenced by the Christian revelation—this increasingly fruitless search for victims has become a grotesque travesty of the Christian message. The victimage mechanism has been turned upside down; it marches on, but in reverse, as it were, facing backward in order not to see the sacrifice of the saving victim, i.e., Christ. But even in its refusal of Christ, the modern secular attitude is forced to acknowledge the truth: the sacrificial victim can no longer be seen in the old way, namely, as that which must be eliminated in order for everybody else to be saved. Now we cannot help knowing that killing victims is bad, that sacrificial victims are scapegoats (in the modern sense of the word), so we search constantly for innocent victims in order to save them from their evil persecutors, so that we can save ourselves by saving them. We depend on victims as much as ever; without saving victims and persecuting persecutors, we would feel defenseless, we would not know how to relieve our own anxiety. But we have adapted our tactics and language to pay lip service to the truth. We are all now on the side of victims; nobody ever sees him- or herself in the role of the old sacrificer. The place of the victim used to be a hellish place; everybody distanced himself from it. It is now, in our still sacrificial eyes, the only safe place to be.

In the popular language of the day, we clearly "identify" with the victims, we "feel" for the victims. And we become profoundly scandalized at their fate—just as Peter became scandalized when Christ announced to the disciples that he had to go to Jerusalem, suffer at the hands of the authorities, and be killed. "That is never going to happen" while I am here, said

Peter. Christ's reaction is of special relevance today: *vade post me Satana scandalum es mihi quia non sapis ea quae Dei sunt sed ea quae hominum* (Matthew 16:23). Peter is scandalized, petrified, and appears as a scandal, a stumbling block, a satanic trap, in front of Christ. And that is exactly what Christ tells him: "You have become a scandal to me, you want to do Satan's work; do not stand in God's way, but get behind me, follow me." This is also why Christ said to the women in Jerusalem, "Do not cry for me, cry for yourselves and for your children." It seems to me we cannot have a clearer warning against our modern scandalized "identification" with the sacrificial or scapegoat victim. Such an identification is a trap; we are *not* the victim, we are the persecutors. Only Christ's revelation of the innocence of the victim is authentic, truthful, not a trap. The persecutors, by definition, never see the innocence of their own victim. To the extent that the innocence-killing violence that we see scandalizes us, we do Satan's work, not God's work. In the universal sacrificial drama revealed by Christ, our role is that of the persecutors. We are also victims only to the extent that we do not really know what we are doing. We have really been duped by Satan—that is to say, by the victimage mechanism itself. This is why Christ's revelation is a call for repentance, not a call to arms in a satanic search for persecutors of victims that we desperately want to save.

This is also why the "overwhelming scourge" still looms as an apocalyptic threat, even though it may no longer be in the form of something like what the prophet envisaged: an immense Assyrian army advancing like an irresistible flood. Its violence may be spread out among a countless multitude of groups or even individuals in ways still unknown, but increasingly driven by sheer violent mimetism, each one technologically capable of inflicting enormous casualties. We do not know, but it would be irresponsible to ignore such a threat, which would be entirely human-made.

John Milbank has argued that "From the perspective of Christian virtue, there emerges to view a hidden thread of continuity between antique reason and modern, secular, reason. This thread of continuity is the theme of 'original violence.' Antique thought and politics assumes some naturally given element of chaotic conflict which must be tamed by the stability and self-identity of reason. Modern thought and politics (most clearly articulated by Nietzsche) assumes that there is *only* this chaos, which cannot be tamed by an opposing transcendent principle, but can be immanently controlled by subjecting it to rules and giving irresistible power to those rules in the form of market economies and sovereign politics."[29]

I agree that one can see such a continuity, not only between "antique reason" and modern secular thought, but from much earlier strata of humanity prior to any development of political thinking. Christianity also teaches us that there was no "ontological necessity" attached to the human violence that founded the human city, the *civitas terrena*. In principle, it did not have to be that way. This is why we talk of "fallen man" and "original sin." But there is no doubt whatsoever that it was that way. "Augustine concedes that this may have been historically the case, but denies any necessity to sinful confusion."[30] I suppose no Christian would have any problem with such an Augustinian reasoning. But we approach the line of intellectual irresponsibility when we claim that the original founding violence is "an essentially imaginary chaos" (Milbank, 398). And I think that the line is crossed when we see something like the following statement:

> [One] must refrain from offering a scientific, explanatory account of the violently sacrificial character of most human cultures. . . . [Their] speaking of a common sacrificial language must simply be accepted as a surd coincidence. If any discipline can elucidate this coincidence further, it is theology, which deciphers it as the dominance of original sin, the refusal of the true God. But this is not really an explanation (sin, in particular, cannot be explained) but only a conceptual redescription, which arises from the contrast with Christianity as a "counter-sacrificial" practice. (Milbank, 398)

"A surd coincidence," that is to say, a dumb, senseless coincidence, which should not even be mentioned; something stupid and unspeakable. At any rate, why speak of it? It was all essentially imaginary—a bad dream, perhaps. However, so many human cultures speaking a common sacrificial language, to use Shakespeare's words, "More witnesseth than fancy's images, / And grows to something of great constancy."[31] Nevertheless, Milbank's testimony is relevant to our purpose. I think he has seen something extremely important, namely, the continuity of the fundamental "theme" (as he calls it) of original violence—we have been calling it the "overwhelming scourge"—throughout the history of political thinking in the West. But guided by his reading of the Christian text, he comes to the conclusion that such a theme cannot be the fundamental one, because there is nothing fundamental, foundational, about human violence, no "ontological necessity." Therefore, that kind of "secular" political thinking is based on a fiction; such an "original violence" has been made up.

What he, incredibly, fails to see is the difference between the historical, physical reality of violence, and what human society from the beginning has done with it in order to make sense of it and deal with it. As Girard has shown, and we have been saying all along, human society turned that violence into a god. It sacralized it, and thereby fictionalized it. That is where the "imaginary" character of original violence lies, in what human beings did with very real and overwhelming violence that truly threatened them with utter annihilation. Through such a sinful and fictionalizing procedure, Cain and his descendants were able to survive and found cities and empires. Otherwise, if the violence that threatened the human city from the beginning was not real, why Christ? *Cur Deus homo*?

CHAPTER 2

The "Overwhelming Scourge" and the *Iliad*

Let us recapitulate: In its prophetic context—that is to say, from the standpoint afforded by God's prophetic announcement about the establishment of the "tested stone," the "precious cornerstone" that the "Lord God is laying in Zion for a foundation"—Isaiah's "overwhelming scourge" acquires universal significance. It points to a widespread social or cultural intuition concerning original violence. In Girardian terms, the "overwhelming scourge" is simply the original mimetic crisis: the collective violence that would have annihilated the human community had it not been expelled and sacralized through the unanimous elimination of the victim-god, the victim who becomes a god as he takes with him, as he dies, the violence that had threatened everybody. He, the victim-god, becomes, in the eyes of the victimizing community, the master or wielder of the overwhelming violence.

From a biblical and, especially, from a Christian perspective, the sacred character of the "overwhelming scourge" can only be seen as an illusion, an idolatrous or satanic illusion. We can no longer believe there is anything transcendental, sacred, God-inspired, about human violence, no matter how overwhelming. But such a biblically inspired view as ours would be something extremely dangerous in a world untouched by, or unrelated to, the Judeo-Christian revelation. And for good reason, of course. Archaic man is right in his belief that unless an untouchable, a sacred distance intervenes between himself and the very violence in which he is engaged, the endless reciprocity of that violence will destroy him. He must both blame it on and transfer it onto something or someone beyond the circle of his everyday living—turn it into an outside or distant danger, which is nevertheless present to him everywhere as a threat.

There is, therefore, a profound wisdom to be learned from the fear of archaic man—the fear that motivates his belief in a violent transcendence. His gods are fiction, but there is a profound and urgent reason why he believes in them. He knows something about human violence that we have foolishly forgotten. He knows that it will overwhelm and overpower him; he knows that he cannot face it directly, because in the end he does not have a chance against it—he will be beaten endlessly by the "overwhelming scourge," as the prophecy announces. His illusion, his "refuge of lies," may not be the best defense, but that is all that archaic man ever had.

We have forgotten the fear of archaic man. And yet Christians ought to know that the old fear was justified, because Christ also announces an incredibly violent apocalyptic end that will test the faith of everybody:

> For then there will be great tribulation, such as has not been since the beginning of the world, no, and never will be. And if those days had not been shortened, no human being would be saved; but for the sake of the elect those days will be shortened. (Matthew 24:21–22)

Furthermore, there can be little doubt about the overwhelming human dimension of such a terrifying violence:

> Nation will rise against nation, and kingdom against kingdom. . . . And then many will fall away, and betray one another, and hate one another . . . . And because wickedness is multiplied, most men's love will grow cold. But he who endures to the end will be saved. (Matthew 24:6–13)

That is not some sort of divine punishment. That is the spiraling reciprocity of human violence feeding on itself, "nation against nation, kingdom against kingdom." That is "wickedness multiplied" as rival moves violently against rival in endless oscillation. If God does not intervene, "no human being would be saved," either physically or spiritually. Not even "the elect" would have the strength to withstand the "wickedness."

But the point is this: Except for the global, planetary dimension of the apocalyptic catastrophe and its destructive power, if viewed simply as human violence unleashed, there is little difference between such violence and the original "overwhelming scourge," the paroxysmal sacrificial crisis from which the archaic sacred emerges. Both are quite capable of destroying every member of the human community. The only fundamental difference between overwhelming human violence at the beginning and overwhelming human violence at the end is, of course, Christ Himself. For all the archaic gods are gone. We can no longer sacralize our own violence. The victimage mechanism is not working as it used to. It has lost its sacralizing power. No matter how violently it tries, it no longer produces any new gods. Our victims, all of which are now marked with the dreadful sign of "persecutor" (since we never see our own persecution as such), no longer turn into gods as we kill them, as they used to in the old days. We keep looking for innocent victims to save from hateful persecutors, onto whom we transfer our own violence. Nevertheless, we cannot avoid looking at our own violence in the face, both for good and for bad. These are the new historical facts, whether you are a Christian or not, whether or not you even believe in God. If you are a Christian, then of course you try to imitate Christ and trust that He will be with you through the end, as He promised—knowing that in the end only He will be able to save you from utter destruction. If you are not, then I suppose you will have to trust exclusively in the power of human reason. So far, the historical record of human reason, all by itself, as a savior from overwhelming human violence has not been good.

Plato, the father of Western philosophy, the inventor of dialectical thinking, made an extraordinary effort to substitute reason, discursive reason, for the ambiguous language of the poets, which was a reflection of the ambivalent, "double-minded" language of ritual sacrifice—that is to say, of the sacred. He wanted to keep the old sacrifices, the victimage mechanism, in place, but subjected to reason, so that one could never confuse a curse for a blessing, as he accused the poets of doing.[1] He was scandalized by the poets' divinization of the victim. If the victim was guilty and unanimously condemned, why—he asked—all the tragic weeping and the wailing when it was killed or expelled? It was blasphemy, he thought, to do such things right next to the sacrificial altar, thereby contaminating the most sacred and pious of all religious acts. That is to say, treating it as if it were a crime, as if they were actually killing the god. A horrible thing to even imagine! The poets, Plato insisted, could not be trusted to properly differentiate between the good and the bad: between the bad violence of a murderous parricide, for example, and the good violence that rightfully kills or expels such a criminal. It was utterly unreasonable to deal with those two things as if they belonged together, as if they were the same.

It is not that Plato wanted to substitute philosophy for sacrificial religion. It was essential to him to maintain the religious horror in the face of violence, and above all, the solid religious unanimity against the crimes of the victim. He was very clear about that: the only way to maintain such a unanimity is for everybody to be convinced of the sacred character of the law that prohibits those crimes. In fact, at some point in his reasoning, these two things, sacredness and unanimity, become practically interchangeable. And then his reasoning became clearly circular: there was unanimity because the broken prohibitions were sacred, and they were sacred because everybody without exception held them to be so.[2] The violent killing of the victim as the source and foundation of the sacred was incomprehensible to Plato. The philosopher could only speak rationally of such a killing if he viewed it as a consequence of the victim's criminal behavior. Without such a premise, the killing was irrational, it did not make any sense. The notion of an irrational, or prerational, prelogical unanimity around the elimination of the victim, a unanimity created by the very violence that kills the victim, was not only beyond the purview of reason in the eyes of the philosopher, but, most importantly, something blasphemous, the most horrendous accusation thrown against the sacred itself. How could sacrifice, the very foundation of law and order, the most sacred of sacred things, be grounded on something so utterly irrational and violent? His was a rational defense of the old sacred against what he perceived as poetic irrationality and blasphemy. But without the revelation of the slain victim as the foundation of the old sacred, Plato's philosophical rationality could not get anywhere. He simply added another, thicker, layer to the old sacred business of hiding the original, foundational killing—to the old business of claiming innocence with all the weeping and the wailing, and sometimes even the blaming of the killing on the knife itself that had just cut the throat of the victim. All those innocence-claiming tactics had become a little too transparent to the rational eye of the philosopher. So he invented a much better way of hiding the (literally) bloody truth.

However, the embarrassing transparency of the old tactics, as well as the irrationality of the poets, carried within it a deeper, unrecognized rationality. The poets were closer to the truth, even though they did not understand it, because they were too terrified by their proximity to it.

In this chapter we will take into account the old poetic wisdom of not asking questions about the guilt or innocence of the sacred victim (a wisdom ignored by Sophocles's Oedipus, for example, for which he paid a heavy price). The old wisdom that said that all such questions are totally out of place before the sacrificial altar. They are very dangerous. You kill the victim because it is your sacred duty to do so. And this duty of yours is sacred because the victim itself is sacred. The entire sacrificial operation is protected against such questions by a sacred shield. Likewise when the terrible violence that threatens the whole group is sacred—which means beyond your capacity to control, unpredictable—the last thing you want or can do is to reason with it, to distinguish between right and wrong, guilt or innocence. The only thing important and urgent is to divert such an overwhelming force away from you. Our approach to the *Iliad*, the other Homeric masterpiece, will be guided by these considerations. If the *Odyssey* taught us to avoid or to hide from the violently overwhelming truth, the *Iliad* will show us how to drive it away.

As is well known, the subject of the *Iliad* is not the Trojan War, of which only a relatively small portion is narrated (actually a few weeks out of a war that lasted more than ten years), and that portion is thrown, as it were, *in medias res*, since it does not include either the beginning or the end of the war. Which means that the poem is not intended as a narrative of the conquest and destruction of Troy by the Greeks. The subject is not the glorious exploits of the old heroes either, even though much of those are indeed factually narrated. It is not even the glorification, in a modern sense, of its central hero, Achilles, who is most definitely not presented as a model of behavior to be followed. The subject of the *Iliad* is clearly stated in a couple of verses right at the very beginning of the poem:

Sing, goddess, the anger of Peleus' son Achilleus
and its devastation, which put pains thousandfold upon the Achaians,

hurled in their multitudes to the house of Hades strong souls
of heroes, but gave their bodies to the delicate feasting
of dogs, of all birds, and the will of Zeus was accomplished
since that time when first there stood in division of conflict
Atreus' son the lord of men and brilliant Achilleus. (1:1–7)[3]

The anger of Achilles and the devastation it caused upon the Achaeans: that is the subject of the poem. A strange subject indeed to a modern reader, because Achilles never lifted a finger against the Achaians, his comrades in arms. It was Hector and the Trojans, their war enemies, who "put pains thousandfold upon the Achaians," just as much pain as the Achaians put upon the Trojans, while Achilles, for the most part, stood by in angry resentment watching the devastation from a distance. It was only when his dear friend and comrade in arms, his *therapon*, his alter ego, is killed, doomed by the same god that will eventually doom Achilles himself, that the terrifying anger of Peleus's son is finally turned toward the Trojans.

What this means is that it does not really matter who does the actual killing. Whether it be the Greek hero himself or the Trojans, what ultimately kills and devastates is this thing called "the anger of Achilles." He, the hero, wields a force that is actually bigger than he is. He possesses it as much as he is possessed by it.[4] It hovers over the battlefield. The hero can direct it against one side or the other, with devastating consequences, like the will of Zeus. He can save the Greeks, or he can doom them. He has all the features of the sacred. Even if all the Greeks were to fall under the Trojan sword, the real cause of their doom would still be the unpropitious "anger of Achilles." The Father of the Gods listens to him:

and [Zeus] himself crashed a great stroke from Ida, and a kindling
flash shot over the people of the Achaians; seeing it
they were stunned, and pale terror took hold of all of them. (8:75–77)

This passage is analyzed by C. Whitman as follows: "The lightning flash which dismays the Achaeans is the direct reflex of Achilles' retirement [in anger]. The action of the god and the inaction of the hero are essentially one" (133–34).

Even from a philological perspective, "the anger of Achilles," the one presented by the poem as its theme at the very beginning, appears to be a special kind of anger, *mênis*:

> Through the preeminent placement of the word *mênis*, the theme of Achilles' anger is singled out by the composition as the most central and hence most pervasive in the Iliadic tradition. Furthermore, the subsequent application of *mênis* is restricted . . . to the anger that Achilles felt over the slighting of his *timé* [honor] at the very beginning of the action. The anger that Achilles felt later over the killing of Patroklos is nowhere denoted by *mênis*. In fact, the only instance where *mênis* applies to heroes rather than gods in the *Iliad* is the mutual anger between Achilles and Agamemnon. (Nagy, 73)

"The anger that Achilles felt later over the killing of Patroklos" will be as destructive to the Trojans as his initial *mênis* was to the Achaeans. In terms of destructive power, there is no difference between one anger and the other. Then what makes the initial one, the root of all the devastation, different and, according to Nagy, uniquely designated by the word *mênis*? The answer may be of interest to mimetic theory: "*mênis* is a *reciprocal* notion" (Nagy, n. 2).[5] In other words, the social context that breeds the kind of anger that threatens the entire group is the reciprocal anger, the rivalry, between Achilles and Agamemnon involving their social ranking, their prestige, their honor. This is the very definition, the essence, of mimetic rivalry. And that is what looms in the eyes of Homer as something overpowering, unstoppable by any human being on his own—the kind of violent force, on the other hand, that makes the hero "equal to the gods," and in consequence, dooms him to death. In fact, at the level of the plot, the "reciprocal," the mimetic, anger of Achilles is preceded and occasioned by the anger, the *mênis*, of Apollo, whose "honor" had also been slighted by Agamemnon, albeit unknowingly. Is it any surprise that Achilles looks so much like Apollo? "Walter Burkert is so struck by the physical resemblance in the traditional representations of the god and the hero . . . that he is moved to describe Achilles as a *Doppelganger* of Apollo" (Nagy, 143). And is it any surprise either that it will be Apollo who eventually will kill Achilles by guiding Paris's arrow to its target? The *Iliad* does not narrate the death of Achilles, but one of the most striking features of Homeric Achilles is the profound sense that the hero has at all times of his approaching death. He knows he is destined to die in battle. He knows he will not go back home to his aging father, Peleus.

Another striking feature of the *Iliad* is the images used to describe the overwhelming power of raging violence in the battlefield. Agamemnon, for example, charges against the Trojans,

As when obliterating fire comes down on the timbered forest
and the roll of the wind carries it everywhere, and bushes
leaning under the force of the fire's rush tumble uprooted,
so before Atreus's son Agamemnon went down the high heads
of the running Trojans . . . . (11:155–60)

Then it is Hector leading the Trojans against the Achaeans,

like a great rolling stone from a rock face
that a river swollen with winter rain has wrenched from its socket
and with immense washing broken the hold of the unwilling rock face;
the springing boulder flies on, and the forest thunders beneath it. (13:137–40)

But above all there is the overwhelming violence of Achilles:

As inhuman fire sweeps on in fury through the deep angles
of a drywood mountain and sets ablaze the depth of the timber
and the blustering wind lashes the flame along, so Achilleus
swept everywhere with his spear like something more than a mortal
harrying them as they died, and the black earth ran blood. (20:490–94)

What is also important for us to emphasize is that the overwhelming character of this violence is inseparable from its sacred character. Whitman was right when he detected something, to use his words, "metaphysical," "absolute" about Achilles's power, to which the symbolism of fire is particularly appropriate. "[The symbolism of fire] is also metaphysical in that it specifically connects the wrath of Achilles with the plan of Zeus, and Achilles himself with the gods. . . . it typifies his extraordinary self-identification with the absolute" (145). But this absolute is a violent absolute, that is to say, absolute violence. What the poem presents is a violence seen as transcending human boundaries, beyond human power to contain. Hence the presence of the gods everywhere. They instigate the violence, they manipulate it constantly, they participate in the battles, favoring one side or the other. If the heroes are demi-gods, we could also say that the gods are demi-humans. And yet they have a distinct role to play; they reveal everywhere the sacred character of the violence in which the humans are engaged.

True, all these divine shenanigans on and above the field of battle are deliberate poetic fictions. But there is the thoughtful awareness of a force stronger than any single human being, which is moving the pen or the voice of the poet. And in such thoughtful awareness, perhaps it is not so much that the force is overwhelming because it is divine, but rather divine because it is overwhelming. There is wisdom and reality behind the fiction. We moderns, in the face of an overwhelming catastrophe that kills millions of people, such as any of our world wars, may ask in anguish, where was God? It is hard for us to see the hand of God behind such an indiscriminate slaughter. But that would be precisely where the Homeric poet would see it.

It is also this constant poetic reminder of the sacred character of the violence that allows the poet to maintain his extraordinary equanimity, his equidistance from the warring contenders. Battles are "the hateful division of Ares" (18:209), and fighting is "the doubtful collision of battle" (18:242). Both sides suffer, and their suffering is equally human. They are both pitied, and their dead are equally mourned.

In this regard, nobody, in my view, has seen more clearly or felt more deeply Homer's justly famous balance between war enemies than Simone Weil in her brilliant analysis of the *Iliad*, to which we must pay some detailed attention: "The *Iliad*," says Weil, "formulated the justice of retaliation long before the Gospels, and almost in the same terms: *Ares is equitable, he kills those who kill.*"[6] The violence that governs the entire development of the *Iliad* is not ultimately controlled by anybody:

> As pitilessly as might crushes, so pitilessly it maddens whoever possesses, or believes he possesses it. None can truly possess it. The human race is not divided, in the *Iliad*, between the vanquished, the slaves, the suppliants on the one hand, and conquerors and masters on the other. No single man is to be found in it who is not, at some point, forced to bow beneath might. (160–61)

Even Achilles, "most terrifying of all men" (18:170), can be terrified by it, as when he runs away from the river god as fast as he can, in fear of his life:

> *Achilleus uprising out of the whirlpool*
> *made a dash to get to the plain in the speed of his quick feet*
> *in fear.* (21:246–48)

And he pleads for help to Father Zeus, feeling like a helpless boy:

> *Father Zeus, no god could endure to save me from the river*
> *who am so pitiful . . .*
> *this is a dismal death I am doomed to be caught in,*
> *trapped in a big river as if I were a boy and a swineherd*
> *swept away by a torrent.* (21:273–83)

Weil is right: "Violence so crushes whomever it touches that it appears at last external no less to him who dispenses it than to him who endures it" (167).

And yet, clearly, not everybody appears to be the same in the light of this violence that overpowers everybody, victors and vanquished alike. One stands out from the rest. In the *Iliad*, that absolute violence has a name. It is called "the anger [or the wrath] of Peleus' son Achilleus." Therefore, more is involved here than simply "necessity and a fickle fortune," as Weil thought (181). There is nothing one can do, at least physically, about blind necessity or blind fortune. But there is definitely something one can do about the overwhelming violence associated with, tied to, the anger of Achilles: one can try and divert it away from oneself, point it toward the enemy. That does not necessarily mean that one hates the enemy. There is no sign of that in Homer. At no point does the poet show any hatred of the enemy. What it means is simply that you want to save yourself, and the only way you can save yourself from the overwhelming violence is to redirect it toward somebody else, to provide a substitute target, since stopping it on your own is obviously out of the question. But how do you manage to get something sacred, transcendental, to move away from you, to spare you? You do what humanity had always done: you sacrifice to it.

This is the whole secret of the *Iliad*. The entire poem is a sacrificial operation. As we said already, its purpose is not to tell the story of the Trojan War or to glorify its heroes in the usual modern sense in which we understand such a glorification. The Homeric hero is never meant to be a guiding beacon, a model, an example to follow. No Greek in his right mind would ever want to be a second Achilles. The very idea would probably terrify him. The poem is, nevertheless, a sacrificial glorification of one hero in particular among all the others. It is a kind of ritual worship, which, historically speaking, must be viewed against the social background of local hero cults. But we have to understand what this worshipful poetic glorification entails. To begin with, it gives the hero a sacred status; it places him next to the gods, which automatically makes him awesome and terrifying, and as a consequence, also triggers the demand for sacrifice, which is the only proper and safe way to approach the sacred. Now, what the poet—that is, the poetic sacrificer—sees through the sacrificial lens, as we know already, is something irreducibly ambivalent: on the one hand something worthy of glory, *kleos*, poetic immortality, and on the other, something extremely dangerous, which must be expelled, kept at a distance. The "best of the Achaeans" is also the most dangerous, the most terrifying, and the most polluting. Homeric Achilles is not there to defend something like "the cause" of the Achaeans. He is there, he is being worshiped, poetically glorified, so that he can save the Achaeans from that terrifying violence which he, himself, embodies, carries, represents. Only he can save the Achaeans, because he is also the one who terrifies them. The Trojan War simply provides the scenario in which this immemorial, and universally ritualized, sacrificial salvation is poetically illustrated, so to speak.

But he to whom the sacrifice is offered is also the one being sacrificed, even if only symbolically, through a substitute. The victim "offered" to the sacred being always stands in place of that same sacred being. In the poetic sacrifice offered to the heroic warrior, it could be said that every man killed in the narrated battle is a sacrificial victim standing in place of the great and terrifying sacred hero. It is therefore no surprise that perceptive critics, who otherwise show no awareness of the sacrificial character of the *Iliad*, notice, for example, that "the most fundamental aspect [of the Hellenic hero is] that the hero must experience death. The hero's death is the theme [?] that gives him his power—not only in cult but also in poetry. We as readers of Hellenic poetry can still sense it" (Nagy, 9). James Redfield, in his Introduction to Nagy's cited work, shows no hesitation in stating that "The *Iliad* is a story about the death of its hero, even though Achilles does not actually die in the story" (x). To which I would only add that "the death of its hero" is a sacrificial death.

From representing the god, standing in place of the god, to being godlike, and looking like the god at whose altar the victim is killed, is just one very small step. That explains, for example, the extraordinary physical resemblance between Achilles and Apollo in Greek art, which we have already mentioned. The plastic arts, as could only be expected, also reflect the sacrificial mentality.

But we have a stunning confirmation of the sacrificial mentality that structures the entire *Iliad*, in the middle of the poem. I am referring, of course, to the death of Patroklos, Achilles's dearest friend, his companion, his *therapon*, who is actually wearing Achilles's armor, looking exactly like Achilles, when he is killed. This is what Nagy says about the word *therapon*:

> As Nadia Van Brock can show, *therapon* had actually meant something like "ritual substitute" at the time it was borrowed into Greek from Anatolia . . . . To paraphrase Van Brock, the Hittite word designates an entity's *alter ego* ("un autre soi-même"), a projection upon whom the impurities of this entity may be transferred. She goes on to cite a Greek reflex of these semantics in the Iliadic application of *therapon* to Patroklos . . . we can see from the contexts where Patroklos is *therapon* of Achilles . . . that the force of the word goes far beyond the dimensions of "warrior's companion." (292)[7]

Cedric Whitman is perfectly explicit about the prophetic and tragic significance of Patroklos's uniquely close ties to Achilles:

> The death of Patroclus is a shadow play of the death of Achilles, a montage of one image upon another, emphasizing with mysterious inevitability the causal relationship between Patroclus' fall and the final stage of Achilles' tragedy. When Achilles' crest drops from Patroclus' head and is stained with dust for the first time in its history, Achilles is already death-devoted, already dead. (201)

However, what these critics and many others tend to forget, perhaps a bit carried away by the poetic force of the narrative, is that Homer is not primarily interested in the poetic beauty, or the metaphysical significance, of

Achilles's tragic death or its poetic anticipation. Death, violent death, is not what Homer wants to meditate about or beautify poetically; death is what he wants to avoid if at all possible. Death is not pretty, or profound, or anything of the sort. In the *Iliad* it is always shallow, horrible, and ugly. It is all those corpses on the battlefield trampled on by horses and chariots, on which dogs and all kinds of birds feed. It obliterates everything that is beautiful. Homer prefers life deeply. His religious and sacrificial understanding of what he is doing gives the poem a sobering seriousness, which most modern, simply literary interpretations badly miss. It is the same kind of seriousness that Auerbach saw in the Old Testament but missed in the *Odyssey*.

Simone Weil's interpretation is, to the best of my knowledge, the only one that avoids the danger of what I might call literary superficiality. She sees the unbelievable violence and destruction in the *Iliad* with the same clarity and horror that Homer presents it. But "such an accumulation of violences would be cold," or "a dismal monotony," if it were not because of its "tender bitterness," and what she calls "moments of grace":

> Such moments of grace are rare in the *Iliad*, but they suffice to make what violence kills, and shall kill, felt with extremest regret.
>
> And yet such an accumulation of violences would be cold without that accent of incurable bitterness which continually makes itself felt. . . . It is this which makes the *Iliad* a unique poem, this bitterness, issuing from its tenderness, and which extends, as the light of the sun, equally over all men. . . . Nothing precious is despised, whether or not destined to perish. The destitution and misery of all men is shown without dissimulation or disdain. . . . The victors and the vanquished are shown equally near to us, in an equal perspective, and seem, by that token, to be the fellows as well of the poet as of the auditors. (176–77)

But not even she realized fully the price that men in the *Iliad* must pay to "might" (*la force*), to sacred, overwhelming violence, in order to give life and whatever is precious in life a chance of survival, even if only a tenuous one. She never saw the role of the sacrificial victim. This becomes apparent in her treatment of Patroklos, whose death is the pivot on which the entire action of the poem turns, since that is the sacrifice that will redirect the wrath of Achilles away from the Achaeans and toward the Trojans.

"In a certain way," says Weil, "Patroclus occupies the central position in the *Iliad*, where it is said that: 'he knew how to be tender toward all'" (173). Which is true; but if she had understood the sacrificial character of Patroklos's death, she would not have failed to notice the similarity between the sacrifice of the gentlest and most compassionate man among the Achaeans and the sacrifice of Christ—since she also believed that "the Gospels are the last and most marvelous expression of Greek genius, as the *Iliad* is its first expression" (180).

However, had she noticed the similarity, she would have also seen the radical difference between the two. She would have noticed, first of all, that the Patroklos whose death saved the Greeks from the wrath of Achilles was no longer the tender and gentle creature that he had been prior to that crucial moment. This is how Cedric Whitman describes the change:

> When he put on the armor of Achilles, a great change came over him. The gentlest man in the army becomes a demon-warrior, who drives the Trojans headlong from the ships, slays the redoubtable Sarpedon, utters proud, insulting speeches over his fallen enemies, and sets foot on the ramparts of Troy itself. . . . He even is given new epithets at the climactic moments: elsewhere his name is modified only by his patronymic or by *hippeus*, "knight"; but when he tussles with Apollo, "he is equal to a god," and the epithet is repeated just before Apollo destroys him. (200)

This transformation of gentle Patroklos into a violent "demon-warrior" is absolutely fundamental. The sacrificial victim, the victim that is intended to push the terrifying sacred violence away, *must be of the same violent nature as the terrifying sacred violence itself.* It bears repeating: the victim is a stand-in for that sacred violence, an image of it. It is killed on the altar of a god who looks just like it. For the unspeakable and terrifying secret of this sacrificial operation is that when you kill the victim, you are also killing the god. The killing of the victim-god generates the transcendent sacred, and the sacred, in turn, sacralizes the killing.

There is no place at all in this violent circularity for tenderness, compassion, innocence—for anything that could be more or less associated with gentle Patroklos. None of that could be assimilated into the sacrificial system that would turn the wrath of Achilles away from the Greeks. In fact, it is much more than that: an obviously innocent sacrificial victim—that is to say, a victim who, *qua victim*, would appear as not deserving to be killed—would not only be a contradiction in terms, it would be taken as sheer blasphemy.[8] The sacrificial community would be terrified by such a spectacle. Plato would be scandalized: What god could possibly accept such a victim! What would such a blasphemous sacrifice say or imply about the most sacred of sacred things? That would be Plato's immediate reaction. The system is not designed, as it were, to handle innocent victims. Only victims who can be blamed for the same violence or calamity for which they are also supposed to be a remedy, can work within the system. The victim, by sacrificial definition, is contaminated by the same violence that threatens the community; it is a carrier of impurities. The question of individual guilt and responsibility is totally irrelevant here. The victim has no individuality other than the one assigned to it by the sacrificial system itself, by its subjacent and unquestioned unanimity. From the perspective of sacrificial rationality, a pure, uncontaminated victim, like Christ, does not make any sense.

Christ's sacrifice, if allowed to stand, would blow the system to pieces. This is what Simone Weil never saw. The subjugation of a human being to "might"—to sacralized, overwhelming, reciprocal violence; in short, to the sacrificial system—is even more terrible than she imagined. For though the granting of a transcendental sacred status to reciprocal human violence opens the possibility for equanimity, for viewing all rivals as equally subject to the same kind of violence, hence viewing everybody as equally human, and equally suffering, *for that very same reason the internal logic of the system denies any fundamental relevance, any transcendental significance, to all those "moments of grace" of which Weil spoke.* She was indeed right to speak of a bitter tenderness. But I am not sure she fathomed the depth of that bitterness. For in the final analysis, the sacrificial system as such, in itself, offers no hope at all for tenderness in any of its forms. And all that the poet can do is to lament such hopelessness—in other words, to console himself poetically. For there is no other kind of consolation open to him. As King Alkinoös of the Phaecians told Odysseus: "The gods spun the destruction of peoples, for the sake of the singing of men hereafter" (8:579–80). But even this consolation, the poetic lament, is in the service of the sacrificial system. Because, inevitably, the lament claims for itself an undeserved innocence. It washes its hands of the blood of the victim—a victim without which the poem itself would not exist. In a most literal sense, gentle Patroklos must be sacrificed in order for his gentleness to be poetically celebrated. Therefore, even the poetic lament, with all its genuinely tender bitterness, cannot escape the sacrificial circularity.

Pity in the face of the victim that must be struck at that very moment is the only kind of pity that can be integrated, that can be meaningful, within the sacrificial system. Pity mixed with fear and terror, as is only appropriate in the presence of the sacred, in the presence of absolute violence. This pity is not meant to move anybody to save the victim from its cruel fate. On the contrary, the victim is pitied precisely because its fate is absolutely inevitable; because there is absolutely nothing that anybody can or should do to prevent it. Any attempt to prevent it, to save the victim, would be looked upon with the deepest kind of horror. Why then a useless pity? we may ask. But it is not useless sacrificially speaking. It serves to distance the sacrificers from the killing, to wash their hands of it, while acknowledging the transcendental character of the force that makes the sacrifice necessary and inevitable; pitying the victim is a way to transfer the responsibility for the sacrificial violence onto the victim itself. When the victim is killed or expelled, that responsibility goes with it as well. Or to put it in well-known Aristotelian terms, pity and fear are "purged"—purged of all the impure accretions that their contact with sacred violence has produced. Once this fearful pity has been purged, everybody can go home, so to speak, feeling refreshingly clean and innocent. All poetically inspired pity can only be this kind of sacrificial, cathartic pity, or a variation thereof. It is definitely not Christian pity. The Gospels are not "the last and most marvelous expression of Greek genius," as Simone Weil thought.

Nevertheless, the sacrificial system whose boundaries Homer never did or could cross, did not require him to place the emphasis he did place on Patroklos's gentle and compassionate character, or his constant and sincere regret over the destruction of what is best and dearest to human beings: love between parents and children, conjugal love, love between comrades in arms, etc. There is no need to doubt the sincerity of the poet in this regard. But, once again, the fundamental difference with Christian sympathy and compassion is hope. There is hope at the most fundamental and transcendental level in the Gospels, at the sacred level; there is hope that "might," overwhelming violence, will not prevail in the end, will not overwhelm the soul completely. There is no such hope in the *Iliad*. But if there is no hope, how can there be "grace"?

Weil tells us that "[Men] can only appear to elevate themselves above human misery by disguising the rigours of destiny in their own eyes, by the help of illusion, of intoxication, or of fanaticism. Unless protected by an armour of lies, man cannot endure might without suffering a blow in the depth of his soul. Grace can prevent this blow from corrupting the soul, but cannot prevent its wound" (182). But what could the corruption of the soul be if not despair, infinite despair? And how can despair be prevented if there is no hope, real hope, which means trust in something both real and beyond the reach of "might"? In Weil's own words, in a later essay, "It is impossible to accept [the] death of the soul unless one possesses another life in addition to the soul's illusory life, unless one has placed one's treasure and one's heart elsewhere . . . , in the hands of our Father who is in secret."[9] Where would Homer place his heart and treasure? It seems to me that Weil is projecting into the *Iliad* the spirit of the Gospels, and then turning everything around and seeing the Gospels as the last expression of the spirit of the *Iliad*.

"Unless protected by an armour of lies, man cannot endure might without suffering a [devastating] blow in the depth of his soul." How true! And that is exactly what Homer did in the *Iliad*, as we already saw that he did in the *Odyssey*. The poem itself is his "armour of lies," his protection. He lends his poetic voice to the overwhelming devastation in order to protect himself from the overwhelming devastation. He substitutes an incredibly realistic and detailed, but totally fictitious devastation in order to protect himself from the real one that he senses intuitively behind any form of violence. The poetic devastation is fictitious not by accident, but by design and ultimate purpose. Even if the poet, if we may imagine the impossible for a moment, had access to, could see, the real thing, he would still have substituted his poetic construct for it. He would have made it look very much like the real thing, not in order to tell the truth, but in the hope that his fiction, his lie, could pass for the truth. As we already saw in our analysis of the *Odyssey*, the whole point was to trick the truth, to snare it, not to reveal it. In spite of what Weil thought, there is reason to believe that the poetic spirit who composed the *Odyssey* was the same one that composed the *Iliad*.

CHAPTER 3

Simone Weil: Between Homer and Christ

What we have said already about Simone Weil and the *Iliad* should give us a sense of the depth of her vision. At first sight, though, her view of the Gospels, and in particular Christ, as the culmination of the Greek genius may appear rather preposterous. And I have no doubt that in the end, such a view is indeed seriously mistaken. But that does not mean that the two things bear no relationship with each other, if we manage to look at the relationship from the proper perspective. For I do not think that Homer could have understood Christ within the sacrificial parameters of his thinking. He would have surely misinterpreted him. But there is no doubt that what Homer says acquires a deeper significance from a Christian perspective. For it is true that "Whoever does not know just how far necessity and a fickle fortune hold the human soul under their domination cannot treat as his equals, nor love as himself, those whom chance has separated from him by an abyss," as Weil says in "The *Iliad* . . ." (*Simone Weil Reader*, 181). Whether the *Iliad* is such an expression of loving others, even your enemy, the "one whom chance has separated from you by an abyss," as one loves oneself is an entirely different matter.

To repeat, the *Iliad* is the poem of "might," or "power," *le poème de la force*. And this power is so overwhelming both to the victors and the vanquished that "it appears at last external" to both. "So the idea was born of a destiny beneath which the aggressors and their victims are equally innocent, the victors and the vanquished brothers in the same misfortune" (167–68). This is very interesting. You begin with the view of a violence so powerful that its destructive force cannot really be controlled by anybody. But as soon as the idea dawns on everybody that they are indeed dealing with a supernatural, a transcendent "destiny," the concurrent idea also appears that they are all, in fact, innocent, because they are all "brothers in the same misfortune." So ideally the basis is established for a possible reconciliation. The question is, how do they actually get to such a reconciliation? For the contenders are still fighting with one another. What is the only thing missing in Weil's scenario? Obviously, the victim.

Weil's "destiny" is the exact equivalent of Girard's violent sacred, *un pouvoir immense et invisible*, a violent "omnipotence," which must be kept at bay, "external," on the outside, through the elimination of a victim, which appears to embody such a destructive omnipotence. The Iliadic war society that Weil contemplates is a society visited by the devastating "destiny," as she calls it. The question is, how will they get rid of such a terrifying visitor; how will they keep it "external," in its sacred transcendence, so that the possible reconciliation can actually take place?

I think she saw quite accurately that the view of human society, of humanity, reflected in the *Iliad* rests on the "external," transcendent character of a violence that equalizes everybody because it victimizes everybody equally. But what she saw were the effects of an underlying sacrificial operation—the sacrificial operation that structures the poem, that is the poem: the reconciling effect, the equanimity, the tender bitterness. But she did not see the sacrificial operation itself, the sacrificial trick, the hidden, fictional, arbitrary moment that makes those effects possible. The truth is that the overpowering violence does indeed equalize everybody in a terrifying way. The fiction comes in when one is arbitrarily made a little more "equal" than the rest, a little more infused with the terrifying violence. As the undifferentiating scourge floods everything, one head is made to stand out and take the blame. In the *Iliad* the one who stands out is Achilles. The scourge bears his name. It is his anger. This is why he is sacred and is destined to die. But before he dies, his anger, the scourge, has to be diverted toward the enemy, for which another victim is needed, who must be as close as possible to the victim-hero and also look like him—in other words, his *therapon*, his sacrificial substitute, Patroklos.

She did not see the sacrificial operation, and yet she intuited the role of the victim. Not so much in this essay of hers on the *Iliad*, but in a later and equally important one entitled "The Love of God and Affliction" ("L'amour de Dieu et le malheur"), which is clearly related, though not explicitly by her, to what she had said about "might" and its effect on the human soul. "Might" can cause a man to become "afflicted," because "affliction is a pulverization of the soul by the mechanical brutality of circumstances. The transformation of a man, in his own eyes, from the human condition into that of a half-crushed worm writhing on the ground" (*Simone Weil Reader*, 462). And this looks exactly like the sort of thing that overwhelming "might" can do to a man's soul.

Affliction is not just suffering: "In the realm of suffering affliction is something apart, specific and irreducible. It is quite a different thing from simple suffering. It takes possession of the soul and marks it through and through with its own particular mark, the mark of slavery."[1] To begin with, there is a social component in affliction: "The social factor is essential. There is not really affliction where there is not social degradation or the fear of it in some form or another" (441). Eric O. Springsted, author of "An Introduction to the Life and Thought of Simone Weil,"[2] recently posted the following description of "affliction" on the Internet:[3]

> Affliction, while including physical suffering, is chiefly a matter of social humiliation, a ceasing to count in anyone's eyes, including one's own. Power [i.e., "might"] simply burns itself into the soul, making the soul more and more an object of other people's actions, no longer the subject of one's own.

The afflicted soul, even though it may be innocent, feels in its very core all the guilt and defilement that should attach to the soul of a criminal but actually does not: "Everything happens as though the state of soul appropriate for criminals had been separated from crime and attached to affliction" (*Simon Weil Reader*, 442). The afflicted man is made to bear the evil that attaches to "the heart of the criminal without being felt there." Then she proceeds to illustrate what she is saying with an example that leaves no room for doubt about the status of the afflicted man as a victim of the social victimage mechanism:

> Men have the same carnal nature as animals. If a hen is hurt, the others rush up and peck it. The phenomenon is as automatic as gravitation. Our senses attach to affliction all the contempt, all the revulsion, all the hatred which our reason attaches to crime. Except for those whose whole soul is inhabited by Christ, everybody despises the afflicted to some extent, although practically no one is conscious of it. (443)

It is hard not to think here of the biblical Servant of Yahweh in Isaiah:

> *He was despised and rejected by men;*
> *a man of sorrows, and acquainted with grief;*
> *and as one from whom men hide their faces*
> *he was despised, and we esteemed him not.* (Isaiah 53:3)

Christ and Job, "a just man as perfect as human nature can be; more so, perhaps, if Job is not so much a historical character as a figure of Christ," are the two archetypal figures of affliction. "As regards affliction, all that departs from this model is more or less tainted with falsehood" (442).

It is regrettable that Weil did not meditate on affliction in the context of what she had said about might in her essay on the *Iliad*. For that would have been the proper place for such a meditation, since in the presence of might, abandoned to a violent "destiny" that pays no attention whatsoever to the individual, affliction should emerge visibly everywhere under the sympathetic eye of the poet, and together with it we should also see, exposed as something blameworthy, the social revulsion, the general contempt mixed with fear—instinctive, irrepressible fear felt toward the afflicted man, the "one from whom men hide their faces." Had she done that, she might have realized something of great significance: there is no explicit evidence of affliction in the *Iliad*, nothing at all resembling biblical Job, or the Servant of Yahweh. If anything, what we see is actually the very opposite of what we see in the Bible. There is one man in the *Iliad* who is clearly the object of such general contempt and revulsion: Thersites,

> *the ugliest man who came beneath Ilion. He was*
> *bandy-legged and went lame on one foot, with shoulders*
> *stooped and drawn together over his chest, and above this*
> *his skull went up to a point with the wool grown sparsely upon it.* (2:216–20)

Clearly one "from whom men hide their faces," Thersites bears the typical marks of the victim of which Girard has spoken. If there is one candidate in the entire poem for the role of a Job or of a Servant of Yahweh, to judge by the reaction of people around him, this would be it. But if we are to believe Homer, the unfortunate creature fully deserved what he got. He was really disgusting, Homer tells us. Everybody hated him, and rightly so. Everybody laughed, "each man looking at the man next him," in perfect connivance, when Odysseus "dashed the sceptre against his back and shoulders," and the ugly creature "sat down again, frightened, in pain, and looking helplessly about" amid the hilarious uproar. Achilles, more than anybody else, hated him. He seemed to be, in fact, the archetypal antihero, the anti-Achilles—or, if one prefers, the hidden side of Achilles, the hateful side of the hero-victim destined to die, and to carry with him all the sacred pollution that has contaminated the group. If Thersites was an afflicted man, nobody around him saw his affliction, least of all Homer. Homer was part of the crowd. He saw what the crowd saw.

Simone Weil would have looked in vain for any evidence of affliction, as such. There is nothing in the *Iliad* that comes even close to what we find in Isaiah 53, the despised and rejected servant of Yahweh, who does not deserve to be so despised and rejected. In the *Iliad*, in theory the ideal place for the exposure of affliction, one can find no trace of it, even though there is plenty of suffering.

Which is really no surprise. Because, in the words of Weil in her later essay, "The Cross of Christ is the only source of light that is bright enough to illumine affliction. . . . Any man, whatever his beliefs may be, has his part in the Cross of Christ if he loves truth to the point of facing affliction rather than escape to the depths of falsehood" (463).

And this brings us to what is perhaps the most significant feature of affliction, or, as we might also call it, the existential face of the sacrificial victim, namely, its intimate association with falsehood:

> Falsehood and affliction are so closely linked that Christ conquered the world simply because he, being the Truth, continued to be the Truth in the very depth of extreme affliction. Thought is constrained by an instinct of self-preservation to fly from the sight of affliction, and this instinct is infinitely more essential to our being than the instinct to avoid physical death. (457)

This would explain something like Oedipus's horror of himself, as he sees himself the cause of all the pollution in the city, when he, in utter despair, gouges out his own eyes, and calls on everybody to throw him out in order to spare them the unbearable horror of such a sight as he. Oedipus, blind and unsightly, surrounded by people who "hide their faces from him," offers the perfect picture, the perfect symbol, of the human attitude in the face of affliction, of which Weil speaks.

Incidentally, there is something that both Oedipus and Thersites have in common: they both limp. In fact, if we could survey the opinion of all those who, absolutely terrified, hid their faces from Oedipus, about Oedipus's physical appearance, we might easily get a rather monstrous picture, either terrifying or repulsive, like Thersites, or a combination of both. What we would not get is the truth. The picture we have imagined of blind Oedipus surrounded by those who hide their faces from him could be titled "The Hiding of the Truth."

Nobody wants to see, or is capable of seeing, that kind of truth—except Christ, or because of Christ. I fully agree with Simone Weil in this. Christ is the one who does not hide his face from any Oedipus or any Thersites; the one who sees, and who reveals, the terrible, the overwhelming, violence involved in this truth-hiding operation, the direct link between what Weil calls "might" and the mythical, collective creation of all the Thersiteses and Oedipuses of the world. And, of course, all the Achilleses and Odysseuses. Christ is the one who sees through all mythico-poetic representations and reveals the truth that they have always hidden. If it is true that "When thought finds itself, through the force of circumstance, brought face to face with affliction it takes immediate *refuge in lies*, like a hunted animal dashing for cover" (*Simon Weil Reader*, 457), what else could the *Iliad* be but such a *refuge in lies*? To repeat what we have said already, Christ cannot be a continuation of the genius who created the *Iliad*, because he is precisely the one who sees through the *Iliad* and reveals what the *Iliad* hides. Except for Christ, Simone Weil would have never discovered the human affliction of which she so brilliantly and profoundly speaks. Homer lied, like almost everybody else, in the face of affliction. As we have seen, the only precedents to the shining visibility of Christ's affliction in the Gospels are to be found in the Jewish Bible, that is to say, in the Old Testament.

In view of everything she says in her later essay on affliction, we can no longer attach much credibility to what she says about the Greeks toward the end of her previous essay on the *Iliad*:

> Particularly rare is a true expression of misfortune: in painting it one almost always affects to believe, first, that degradation is the innate vocation of the unfortunate; second, that a soul may suffer affliction without being marked by it, without changing all consciousness in a particular manner which belongs to itself alone. For the most part the Greeks had such strength of soul as preserved them from self-deception. For this they were recompensed by knowing in all things how to attain the highest degree of lucidity, of purity and of simplicity. (181)

It is hard to imagine that she could have written that after her meditations on "The Love of God and Affliction." So perhaps we should say something at this point regarding Simone Weil's explicitly declared hostility toward the Hebrews. Because such hostility is so closely linked to her unbounded admiration for the Greeks, and for the *Iliad* in particular, "the only veritable epic of the western world" (180).

In general, with a few exceptions, she did not like the Old Testament at all, in particular the Book of *Joshua*, with all the serial slaughtering of people and the burning down of cities. There can be little doubt indeed that the God who commands Joshua to do all those things is a rather primitive God, and a very jealous one, as Joshua himself tells his people. He admits no competition. He is the one and only. But precisely because of that, He is like no other god, and his people know exactly what to expect. Bloody as they may be, his commands are quite clear, and they involve all kinds of rules of conduct. If they keep them, He will be on their side; if they do not, He will be against them. The Homeric gods, on the other hand, are totally unpredictable. Nobody knows how this or the other god may react in any given situation.

There are no rules of the game, no specific commands. Therefore, the first, and about the only, thing that the Homeric man can do is to try to gain their favor in whatever way he can. The Homeric man will worship whatever he has to worship to keep himself out of harm's way. It would be counterproductive to limit one's worshiping choices. One never knows the kind of trouble one may be facing tomorrow. This intimate association between threatening violence and the sacred is at the root of polytheism. But the Homeric man is sure of one thing: whatever the trouble may be, it is sacred; it comes from a god who, for some reason of which he may be totally unaware, is angry at him. In his final analysis, trouble does not really come from the human enemy who may be about to strike. The enemy is only the god's instrument to get at him. And he is too fearful of the gods to really hate his enemy, even though he may be eager to sacrifice as many enemies as he can! Which is the kind of situation that, seen from the outside, may fool somebody with a Christian mind into believing he is watching an example, if not of Christian love, of Christian understanding of the humanity of the enemy. Is that not what happened to Simone Weil? And yet she must have known that none of the Greek heroes would have hesitated for a moment in offering a multitude of Trojans, as many as necessary, in holocaust to any god, if he thought it would propitiate the god. In fact, something like that is what Achilles does with "the twelve young men [he took] alive from the river . . . bewildered with fear like fawns" (21:27–29) to be sacrificed at the funeral of Patroklos.

The God of Joshua commands his people to do many violent and bloody things. But he is not identical with the violence that He commands. Eventually, in the course of the history of the Jewish people, this separation between God and sacrificial violence will increase, as we have already seen in the case of Isaiah. There is no such separation between violence and the Homeric gods. They are the gods of the violence that threatens the people—its sacred side. Whatever that violence may happen to be at the moment, the gods will metamorphose themselves into it.

In a lesser-known essay of hers entitled "Les trois fils de Noé et l'histoire de la civilisation méditerranéenne," for which I have found no English translation, Simone Weil wrote:

> À la révélation surnaturelle Israël opposa un refus, car il ne lui fallait pas un Dieu qui parle à l'âme dans le secret, mais un Dieu présent à la collectivité

> nationale et protecteur dans la guerre. Il voulait la puissance et la prospérité. Malgré leurs contacts fréquents et prolongés avec l'Égypte, les Hébreux restèrent imperméables à la foi dans Osiris, dans l'immortalité, dans le salut, dans l'identification de l'âme à Dieu par la charité. Ce refus rendit possible la mise à mort du Christ. Il se prolongea après cette mort, dans la dispersion et la souffrance sans fin. (*Attente de Dieu*, 166)[4]
>
> [Israel refused to accept the supernatural revelation, because what it wanted was not a God who speaks to the soul in secret, but a God visible to the national community and protector in war. Israel wanted power and prosperity. In spite of their frequent and lengthy contacts with Egypt, Jews remained impermeable to faith in Osiris, in immortality, in salvation, in the union of the soul with God in love. This refusal made possible the execution of Christ. It continued after his death, throughout the dispersion and endless suffering.]

In the same essay, she explains that Herodotus and others believed that religion originated in Egypt. And this is confirmed by "a splendid page in Ezechiel."[5] Most of the Greek gods are equivalent appellations of one great god, who ultimately goes back to the Egyptian Osiris (164).

I simply cannot understand why she would think, by implication, that Homeric man did not need or did not want "a God present to the national community and protector in war." As far as the Homeric poems are concerned, there is not the slightest indication of the existence of such a human being. And how could "the Hebrews' impermeability to the faith of Osiris" be responsible for their putting Christ to death? Does that mean that the Egyptians, or the Greeks, their religious descendants, would not have killed Christ? Why would they not do to Christ what they did to Osiris, or to Dionysos? Clearly they would have killed him, as in their stories that tell us that they killed their gods. And if they could have had their way, nobody would have ever known that they had killed an innocent man, that their killing was an injustice, and that they had been told to repent and mend their ways. A strange thing to say, from their point of view; why would they have to repent from killing a god, or the representative of a god, when it was their most sacred duty to do so, when such killing had always been presented as a sacred precedent to be repeated reverently? And as a matter of public utility, why would anybody repent of killing Osiris when even the periodic floods of the Nile, and so many other public benefits, flowed from it? However, had they killed Christ, foolishly thinking that he was another Osiris, they would have been badly disappointed, because the death of Christ does not bring with it directly any social or civilizational benefits. On the contrary, what the death of Christ does is to reveal that society or civilization is not going to be enough to save humanity from its own destructive violence.

In another passage of the same essay, Weil writes the following:

> Ce n'était pas contre l'idolâtrie que le Christ avait lancé le feu de son indignation, c'était contre les pharisiens, artisans et adeptes de la restauration religieuse et nationale juive, ennemis de l'esprit hellénique. "Vous avez enlevé la clef de la connaissance." A-t-on jamais saisi la portée de cette accusation? (167)
>
> [It was not against idolatry that Christ directed the fire of his indignation, it was against the Pharisees, the artisans and adherents to the Jewish national and religious restoration, the enemies of the Hellenic spirit. "You have taken away the key to knowledge." Have we ever grasped the full extent of this accusation?]

Yes, it is true that Christ was not exactly an iconoclast. We do not see him raging against false gods. What he does is to reveal and expose the violence that creates them, the original murder that humanity has kept "hidden since the foundation of the world." He is there not to destroy false images, but the very roots of falsehood. In fact, the only place where this revelation is anticipated, as Girard points out, is "in the great biblical texts and above all in the prophetic books." We have already seen in the text of Isaiah how the prophet attacks not the idols directly, but the "refuge of lies" that houses them.

Girard has dealt with this Gospel passage in detail, and although I do not think he had Simone Weil in mind at the time, what he said is fully applicable to our purpose here. What follows is basically a summary and an adaptation of Girard's words on the subject in *Things Hidden since the Foundation of the World*.[6] But first we must place Christ's words in their context:

> Woe to you [lawyers]! for you build the tombs of the prophets whom your fathers killed. So you are witnesses and consent to the deeds of your fathers; for they killed them and you build their tombs. Therefore also the Wisdom of God said, "I will send them prophets and apostles, some of whom they will kill and persecute," that the blood of all the prophets, shed from the foundation of the world, may be required of this generation, from the blood of Abel to the blood of Zechariah, who perished between the altar and the sanctuary. Yes, I tell you, it shall be required of this generation. Woe to you lawyers! *for you have taken away the key of knowledge*; you did not enter yourselves, and you hindered those who were entering. (Luke 11:47–52)[7]

Obviously Christ cannot make the Jewish scribes and Pharisees specifically responsible for the blood of Abel and of all the prophets "from the foundation of the world," or as we read in the text of Matthew, "all the righteous blood shed on earth." There were no Jews at the time of Abel. Cainite culture is not specifically Jewish. It is simply human. "It therefore looks," in Girard's words, "as though the kind of murder for which Abel here forms the prototype is not limited to a single region of the world or to a single period of history. We are dealing with a universal phenomenon whose consequences are going to fall not only upon the Pharisees but upon this *generation*, that is, upon all those who are contemporary with the Gospels and the time of their diffusion, who remain deaf and blind to the news that is being proclaimed" (*Things Hidden*, 159).

Christ is addressing all human beings through the Pharisees. And he is telling us that we are not only accomplices in the murder of the innocent from the beginning of the world, but also that from the beginning we have been covering up all those murders. That is precisely what tombs do. They hide the dead from view. This is how we hide the murders that our fathers committed: "you build the tombs of the prophets whom your fathers killed." Since time immemorial, nothing has been considered as impious and polluting, in a religious sense, as an unburied corpse. The souls of the dead could not be admitted to Hades unless their bodies were properly, ritually, disposed of: witness the soul of Patroklos in the *Iliad*, or that of Palinurus in the *Aeneid*, to mention two well-known examples. The ultimate outrage that can be inflicted on a fallen enemy is to leave the body unburied; or, to pile outrage upon outrage, to drag it endlessly around, as Achilles does with the body of Hector. But when you bury the body, you also bury—that is to say, you hide—the violence that kills it. Because the burial is a sacrificial act. It sacralizes the body and the violence that kills it—a sacralization that is at the very root and center of the sacrificial system, of the *civitas terrena*. Here is Girard again:

> This act of concealment is essential. The very murders in which the fathers directly took part already resemble tombs to the extent that, above all in collective and founding murders but also in individual murders, men kill in order to lie to others and to themselves on the subject of violence and death. They must kill and continue to kill, strange as it may seem, in order not to know that they are killing. . . .
>
> So we have here a problem of *knowledge* which is always being lost, never to be rediscovered again. This knowledge certainly comes to the surface in the great biblical texts and above all in the prophetic books, but the organization of religion and law contrives to repress it. The Pharisees, who are satisfied with what seems to them to be their success in the religious life, are blind to the essentials and so they blind those whom they claim to be guiding. (*Things Hidden*, 163–66)

In the Gospel of John, this lack of understanding is explicitly associated with the devil:

> Why do you not understand what I say? It is because you cannot bear to hear my word. You are of your father the devil, and your will is to do your father's desires. He was a murderer from the beginning, and has nothing to do with the truth, because there is no truth in him. When he lies, he speaks according to his own nature, for he is a liar and the father of lies. (John 8:43–44)

Jesus is still addressing here the same "generation." But in John, the original murder to which we are accomplices has become universalized. Our father is the original murderer, who is also the original liar. To murder is to lie, and the lie is made sacred so that nobody can touch it. Girard tells us that "N. A. Dahl has demonstrated that calling Satan a homicide is a concealed reference to the murder of Abel by Cain. It is undoubtedly true that Abel's murder in

Genesis has an exceptional importance. But this importance is due to the fact that it is the first founding murder and the first biblical account to raise a corner of the curtain that always covers the frightful role played by homicide in the foundation of human communities" (*Things Hidden*, 161).[8] There are plenty of fratricidal stories in pagan mythology, but none in which the murder is revealed so unambiguously as such, and so clearly condemned, as in the biblical story.

But it is precisely this idea—namely, that Christ's revelation is attached to the Jewish Bible, to the Old Testament, in a special and unique way—that bothered Simone Weil deeply. I think she wanted to save the meaning of Christ's passion from what she considered to be an arbitrary restriction, an obstacle to Christ's universal relevance. This extraordinary Jewish "woman of genius, of a kind of genius akin to that of the saints," as T. S. Eliot is quoted as saying, was radically opposed to the view of the Jewish people as divinely "chosen." So she looked everywhere for parallels and similarities between the Christian revelation and the religious traditions of other people—the Greeks in particular, whom she admired so much.

There is a great insight and an equally great blindness in this view of Simone Weil's. It is true, of course, that Christ's revelation, contained in the story of his public life and the manner of his death and resurrection, if it is universally true, must be related to fundamental religious intuitions and beliefs all over the world. If it is relevant to everybody, it cannot be an alien and incomprehensible truth to anybody. Everybody, each within his or her own cultural tradition, should be able to recognize it. This is particularly true about the Passion, as Girard has pointed out:

> Because it reproduces the founding event of all rituals, the Passion is connected with every ritual in the entire planet. There is not an incident in it that cannot be found in countless instances: the preliminary trial, the derisive crowd, the grotesque honors accorded to the victim, and the particular role played by chance, in the form of casting lots. . . . The final feature is the degrading punishment that takes place outside the holy city in order not to contaminate it. (*Things Hidden*, 167)

And, needless to say, there are also countless instances of gods resurrecting from their ashes, for example, or being brought back to life from some of their bodily parts that had been torn apart, as in the case of Dionysos.[9] It has always been a Christian belief that Christ defeated Satan at Satan's own game, so to speak, surrendering himself into the hands of Satan. In other words, Christ's death followed a universal sacrificial, victimizing pattern. After which, the horror of such a pattern, Satan's pattern, was revealed. What men did to Christ was not what they should have done. And that is precisely what was revealed to them: the injustice, the sinfulness, of it, together with the message that such injustice is what they had been doing from the beginning of the world. The killing of Christ became unavoidable, necessary, not because the killing itself was good, or because it would bring desirable things to earth, like Promethean fire, or because it would help to preserve the benefits of human civilized society. The killing of Christ became unavoidable from the perspective of a loving God—first of all, because there was nothing in human society or civilization that would ultimately save humanity from its own violence, and secondly, because given the fact that all men are sinners, sacrificers, expellers of the truth of their own violence, that was the only way to make them understand, if they wanted to.

The Egyptians and the Greeks would have killed Christ just as the Hebrews and the Romans did, and for exactly the same reasons. Men anywhere would have done the same thing as soon as Christ appeared on the earth, and spoke and acted the way he did. For reasons known only to God, the job fell on the Jews from the beginning, for which they, in turn, have been victimized by the rest of the world, thereby proving that the rest of the world would have done exactly the same thing as the Jews. Had Weil not read Matthew 23:29–30?

> Woe to you scribes and Pharisees, hypocrites! for you build the tombs of the prophets and adorn the monuments of the righteous, saying, "If we had lived in the days of our fathers, we would not have taken part with them in shedding the blood of the prophets."

Girard comments on this passage: "The *sons* believe they can express their independence of the *fathers* by condemning them, that is, by claiming to have no part in the murder. But by virtue of this very fact, they unconsciously imitate and repeat the acts of their fathers. They fail to understand that in the murder of the Prophets people refused to acknowledge their own violence and cast it off from themselves" (*Things Hidden*, 160).

It is also worth mentioning that the idea that all those mythological narratives ultimately, unknowingly, said something about Christ, anticipated Christ in some way, is an old idea. In *Celui par qui le scandale arrive*, Girard tells us that the Byzantines interpreted Sophocles's tragedy *Oedipus the King* as a Christian Passion: "Ils voyaient le Christ dans l'Oedipe, ils voyaient la victime innocente" (142). It is also the idea that moves the greatest Spanish dramatist of the seventeenth century, Calderón, to write so many *Autos sacramentales*, sacramental one-act plays in honor of the Eucharist, with mythological themes and titles such as *El divino Jasón*, *Psiquis y Cupido*, *El sacro Parnaso*, *El verdadero Dios Pan*, *Andromeda y Perseo*, or *El divino Orfeo*. And Calderón, a priest at that time, wrote those plays under the watchful eye of the Inquisition.

This is why, in spite of her incomplete or misleading historical perception of the Greeks, and her arbitrary hostility towards the Hebrews, Simone Weil still had a very profound intuition when she thought and felt deeply that Homer's vision of violence in the *Iliad* was something larger than human, something that overwhelms the human; and when she thought as well that it was something, a "destiny" she called it, intimately connected with Christ's revelation, and even more specifically with Christ's affliction. It seems to me as if she saw the face of the afflicted Christ underneath the crushing weight of Iliadic "might," which I think is the equivalent of the "overwhelming scourge" of which Isaiah spoke. This is also why she saw Homer as some sort of prophet or herald of the spirit of Christ. And, in a certain sense, she was right, of course. Christ's revelation does not make much sense without the presence of the prophetic "overwhelming scourge." If the power of the world is not the power of Satan, why Christ? If human society is not in the grip of a violence that it cannot ultimately control by purely human means, why Christ?

Simone Weil also saw with great depth and lucidity that no human being, unless aided by Christ, can face up to the kind of affliction that made Christ himself sweat blood, without "dashing for cover," without taking "immediate refuge in lies," burrowing "very deep into falsehood." But she failed to see the collective dimension of such falsehood, the social mechanism that fabricates the "refuge of lies" inside of which men hope to escape the overwhelming scourge. In other words, she appears to have been completely unaware of the sacrificial mechanism that created human society and has kept it going from the beginning. She did not see what Girard would see a few decades later.

But perhaps she saw something to which Girard has not paid much attention. I am referring to the very notion of "affliction," which, in my opinion, is the central notion in Simone Weil's understanding of Christ. This is an existential aspect of the Passion and of its revelatory power, which I do not recall ever seeing in the foreground, at the center, of Girard's reflections, even though there are, of course, passing references to Christ's suffering scattered throughout his work.

The Gospels tell us that Christ was deeply anguished, "sorrowful, even unto death" (Matthew 26:38). The intensity of his agony was such that "his sweat became like great drops of blood falling down upon the ground" (Luke 22:44). The three Synoptic Gospels narrate Christ's affliction in detail. They clearly want to emphasize what a horrendous moment this is for Jesus, the Son of Man. Luke even suggests that the bitterness of the chalice that Jesus must take is such that his human strength weakens: "And there appeared to him an angel from heaven, strengthening him." It seems to me that at no other time is the humanity of Jesus so explicitly highlighted as at this moment—not even on the cross. This is the only moment in which we actually see Jesus asking the Father to spare him from what he knows is coming, if at all possible, even though he also prays that the Father's will be done, not his own.

Is it fear? Fear of the approaching physical suffering and the public humiliation? That would not make much sense, as Hilary, one of the Church Fathers, explains, as quoted in Thomas Aquinas's *Catena aurea*:

> I suppose that there are some who offer here no other cause of His fear than His passion and death. I ask those who think thus, whether it stands with reason that He should have feared to die, who banished from the Apostles all fear of death, and exhorted them to the glory of martyrdom? How can we suppose Him to have felt pain and grief in the sacrament of death, who rewards with life those who die for Him? And what pangs of death could He fear, who came to death of the free choice of His own power?[10]

Jesus is "troubled," "sad," "sorrowful even unto death," "in great distress," or "in agony." That is not ordinary fear, and that is not ordinary suffering either. I think that is what Simone Weil called "affliction," which, as she said, "is quite a different thing from simple suffering." "[It] is not a psychological state. . . . Affliction is something which imposes itself upon a man quite against his will" (*Simon Weil Reader*, 462). And as I have already indicated, if we take her existential insights into the nature of affliction as a guide, we can see the place of affliction as the place of the victim, which she did not see as such, of course, because she was not aware of the victimage mechanism.

Jesus's affliction in Gethsemane echoes the words of the Psalmist; for example:

> *Give ear to my prayer, O God*
> . . .
> *I am overcome by my trouble.*
> *I am distraught by the noise of the enemy,*
> *because of the oppression of the wicked.*
> *For they bring trouble upon me,*
> *and in anger they cherish enmity against me.*
> *My heart is in anguish within me,*
> *the terrors of death have fallen upon me.*
> *Fear and trembling come upon me,*
> *and horror overwhelms me.* (Psalm 55:1–5)

From a Girardian perspective, this is clearly the place of the victim: surrounded by enemies, rejected by everybody, as in the case of the Suffering Servant in Isaiah. In fact, the idea that Christ's agony in Gethsemane was caused by the vision of his own disciples abandoning him, as well as the rejection of the Jewish people, his own people, is already present in the interpretation of the Church Fathers, as we can see in the *Catena aurea*. But if he is abandoned by his friends and rejected by his people, that means that he is facing his fate utterly alone. If at this moment of extreme affliction he is bearing "the sins of the world," then he is infinitely alone; fallen humankind in its totality from its victimizing beginning, from the first murder to the last, surrounds him and rejects him. But even that immense solitude does not explain everything. Because at that moment Christ is not only "sorrowful even unto death," he is also being tempted or tested, solicited by temptation. In the midst of his own affliction, he is driven repeatedly to go back to his closest friends to warn them: "Watch, and pray that you may not enter into temptation," which is obviously what he is doing, watching and praying. But who or what is tempting him, what is the nature of the temptation, and what would it mean to yield to it, to enter into it?

We will have to go back to the beginning of the victimage mechanism, which is the beginning of the violent sacred; to that moment in which a universal omnipotence—"an immense and invisible power," to use Girard's expression once again—is invested with a violence that does not really belong to it, because it is the work of man. We have to go back to that moment when human violence—mimetically reciprocal, open-ended, human violence—becomes sacred, properly satanic; the moment, we might say, when Satan acquires his overpowering dominion over all of humanity. Or perhaps we should rather say, the moment when men usurp the power of God and mold it into a violent and tyrannical god of their own making, before whom they then bow in terrified adoration. And all of this usurpation and investing of divine power is done through the killing of the human victim. The creative, nonviolent power of God, omnipresent, immense, and invisible, which was out there when the first humans became humans by opening their eyes to the spirit of the world out there, is turned violently into a satanic look-alike, a false god, through the victim. It is the victim that literally becomes the incarnation of the satanic god, which has become invested illegitimately, unjustly, foolishly, with the spirit of God that was really out there, revealing the world as being *truly* out there. Ironically, tragically, human violence, the violence of a creature made in God's image, would have never been able to divinize itself, to project itself into its own satanic god, without the possibility of usurping, co-opting, the spirit of the real God. The usurper is a liar, of course, a fake; but its power, the power of its lie, is immense, because to all appearances it is God. To repeat Simone Weil's illuminating words, "Christ conquered the world simply because he, being the Truth, continued to be the Truth in the very depth of extreme affliction."

In the midst of the greatest possible affliction, Christ is being tempted by Satan, the tempter, the "liar from the beginning." And Satan tempts him with the humanly irresistible attraction of his lie. For the tempter has two faces, or two sides, that complement each other: on one side it threatens with a violence that appears to be omnipotent because it wears the face of the spirit; on the other, it tempts with a correspondingly irresistible way to escape from such overwhelming violence. This side wears the face of the victim, and it says: "Join the crowd, join everybody else, kill it, acknowledge that I am god." For Satan is the god of the crowd. Even when he speaks in the recesses of the soul, his voice is still the voice of the crowd.

Inside the agony, Satan tempts Christ with a temptation that is fundamentally the same as the one he used when he asked Christ to prostrate himself before him and adore him as god, in exchange for power over all the kingdoms of the world, which he rules. What we now see is the horrendous price that Christ must pay for rejecting Satan, for resisting the power of the human crowd from the beginning till the end. As he resists the satanic power of the crowd, he reveals the affliction of the victim, because he is now in the place of the victim, the foundation of Satan's power. Therefore he is also at an infinite distance from God the Father. Satan's tempting power is now at its peak, because it is in direct proportion to the absence of God. No other human being could have possibly resisted on his own.

To describe how extreme affliction pierces the soul, Simone Weil uses a powerful image, which in her case has a clear mystical dimension, but which can also be adapted to our purpose here:

> When a hammer strikes a nail the shock travels, without losing any of its force, from the nail's large head to the point, although it is only a point. If the hammer and the nail's head were infinitely large the effect would still be the same. The point of the nail would transmit this infinite shock at the place where it was applied.
>
> Extreme affliction, which means physical pain, distress of soul, and social degradation, all together, is the nail. The point of the nail is applied to the very center of the soul, and its head is the whole of necessity throughout all space and time.
>
> Affliction is a marvel of divine technique. It is a simple and ingenious device to introduce into the soul of a finite creature that immensity of force, blind, brutal, and cold. The infinite distance which separates God from the creature is concentrated into a point to transfix the centre of a soul. (*Simone Weil Reader*, 452)

But if "throughout the horror" of this brutal strike the soul maintains its loving orientation towards God, it enters a "marvellous dimension" in which "the soul can traverse the whole of space and time and come into the actual presence of God," because the point at which the brutal piercing strike has fixed the soul is "the point of intersection between creation and Creator . . . the point of intersection of the two branches of the Cross" (452).

What this passage suggests to me is that "the infinite distance which separates God from the creature" would not be an immensely "blind, brutal, and cold" force if it were not also a satanic force, the source of all human affliction—that is to say, if it did not also imply the sacralization or divinization of open-ended human violence, the idol capable of putting on the appearance of the true God, because it originally usurped, co-opted, the spirit of the truth, the spirit of the world that was *truly* out there, in God's creation as it manifested itself to human beings. The point of intersection between Creator and creation would not be such a horrendous affliction for human beings if creation itself had not been perverted.

By maintaining himself totally faithful to the truth and the love of the Father, Christ will not only break the power of Satan over human beings, but he will also restore the spirit of God over His entire creation. Offering man the possibility of freedom from his own violence and restoring the spirit of truth to the world out there are the two sides of the same liberation; or as Saint Paul says in his letter to the Ephesians, "He who descended is he who ascended far above all the heavens, that he might fill all things" (4:10); for he who is grounded in love "may have power to comprehend with all the saints what is the breadth and length and height and depth, and to know the love of Christ which surpasses knowledge" (3:18–19).

The image of the nail with an immensely large head ("the whole of necessity throughout all space and time"), which drives the violence of the strike onto a single point at the very center of the human soul, can be easily translated to a Girardian context: the immense satanic crowd from the first murder on (which has usurped the spirit of God throughout all creation) transfers all its violence onto a single victim, who becomes afflicted at his very core, at the point of his or her radical singularity. This is the point and the moment at which every single human being "takes immediate refuge in lies, like a hunted animal dashing for cover . . . in its terror [burrowing] very deep into falsehood." Everybody runs away from satanic singularity, which means that in the face of affliction, everybody joins the violent crowd. Therefore, here is something else that Christ rescues from the power of Satan, god of the crowd, as He keeps himself faithful to the truth and the love of the Father, by not "taking refuge in lies," in the midst of extreme affliction: the singularity of each and every human individual. The restoration of such a human singularity is also part of the restoration of the spirit of truth to the whole of creation. Christ is the one who can keep the human individual from becoming hopelessly and violently entangled in the mimetic web, which is also the collective and idolatrous "refuge of lies," or, in Girardian terms, the victimage mechanism.

I find this correspondence between the purely existential analysis of Simone Weil and the anthropological and social analysis of Girard quite revealing. Each one illuminates less obvious aspects in the other. Here is another example: the panic-driven "dashing for cover" of which Weil speaks is an existential reaction comparable to the terrifying stepping back before the abyss that Girard finds in some of the Greek tragedians, in Sophocles and Euripides in particular.

The spirit of Greek tragedy—says Girard—does not quite follow the spirit of the mythical story on which it is based at the level of the plot. A successful tragedy inevitably questions some of the traditional assumptions of the mythical legend. For example, Sophocles's *Oedipus the King* comes very close to questioning the basic traditional assumption that Oedipus is the one and only cause of the plague that is devastating the city. As the verbal violence, the reciprocal accusations between Oedipus and Creon, or between Oedipus and Teiresias, escalates, the difference between the characters tends to disappear. Fundamental questions are asked, such as, was the former king, Laius, killed by one, or by many? If by many, then Oedipus is not guilty of parricide, and the sacred oracle was wrong. In fact, this fundamental question (was it one or many?) is never answered explicitly in the text of the tragedy. In the case of Euripides's *Bacchae*, the questioning of the sacred character of Dionysos and of Dionysiac rituals is at the very center of the tragedy and perfectly explicit.

Furthermore, given the fact that a tragic performance is still a sacrificial operation, based on the foundational logic of the victimage mechanism—that is, the unanimous transfer of collective violence onto one victim, who is sacred and, therefore, uniquely different—questioning the uniqueness of the victim, its sacred character (in other words, implying that the choice of the victim is arbitrary) may amount to shaking the pillar that sustains the entire sacrificial edifice, which is the only defense the community has against a violence that it cannot control otherwise, an "overwhelming scourge" that would be devastating. Therefore, at the sight of such an apocalyptic abyss, even the most daring tragedian steps back in panic from a truth that would annihilate him. These are the words of Girard:

> From the very fact that it belies the overt mythological messages, tragic drama opens a vast abyss before the poet; but he always draws back at the last moment. He is exposed to a form of hubris more dangerous than any contracted by his characters; it has to do with a truth that is felt to be infinitely destructive, even if it is not fully understood. (*Violence and the Sacred*, 135)

Archaic religion works as long as the truth on which it rests is not revealed:

> [Religion] protects man as long as its ultimate foundations are not revealed. . . . To remove men's ignorance is only to risk exposing them to an even greater peril. The only barrier against human violence is based on misconception [*méconnaissance*]. In fact, the sacrificial is simply another form of that knowledge which grows greater as the reciprocal violence grows more intense but which never leads to the whole truth. It is the knowledge of violence, along with the violence itself, that the act of expulsion succeeds in shunting outside the realm of consciousness. (135)

Clearly, Girard's intuition confirms that of Simone Weil. The tragedian's panicky step back from "a truth that is felt to be infinitely destructive" is the pre-Christian form of the existential "dashing for cover," or "burrowing deep into falsehood" of which Weil speaks.

The correspondence between the two views seems clear to me, even though the way in which Girard explains the tragedian's panic in *Violence and the Sacred* may be somewhat misleading. And this is why I think so: Is it really true that the dramatic doubt about the uniqueness, the sacred character, of the tragic victim undermines the effectiveness of the sacrificial mechanism? It would seem rational. The problem is that the mechanism functions with complete independence from reason. Indeed, it functions precisely beyond the point at which reason becomes completely powerless, mute, without an answer. To probe the irrationality of the mechanism is to stir the sacred monster from its lair to show its immense superiority and power. I do not think it is quite accurate to say that the sacrificial expulsion "[shunts] outside the realm of consciousness" both "the knowledge of violence" together with "the violence itself." It would be more accurate to say that rational knowledge is simply powerless before an "infinitely destructive truth." In such a situation human reason can only acknowledge its helplessness. And this acknowledgment, in turn, enhances the sacrificial process. Under the rule of Satan human reason is under constant threat to stay within its limits, and never try to interfere with the sacred truth.

But within its sacrificial limits reason can see many things that are true, including the rationally arbitrary character of the sacred victim. It is an error to think that such a rational knowledge endangers the efficiency of the sacrificial system. The system worked, while it worked, not because of what men did not know, but because of what they knew and felt powerless about. They had every reason to believe that they could not control the violence with which they were killing one another. They sacralized their violence because it truly transcended their power. If the victim provided the conduit through which their, otherwise uncontrollable, violence could be expelled, what difference would it make whether or not the victim was chosen in a totally accidental manner? Virgil can teach us a lesson in this regard.

CHAPTER 4

From Virgil to the Modern Era

If human reason alone had ever had the power to undermine the foundation of the victimage mechanism, pagan religion would have disappeared from Greco-Roman civilization before the arrival of Christianity. But pagan reason never had that power. Philosophy and science developed a parallel existence to that of traditional sacrificial religion without changing anything fundamental about it, because, interestingly, there was a generalized feeling that both pursued the same ultimate goal in different ways. Virgil is perhaps the greatest example of such coexistence.[1] These famous verses in the *Georgics* could summarize this whole attitude:

Felix, qui potuit rerum cognoscere causas,
atque metus omnis et inexorabile fatum
subiecit pedibus strepitumque Acherontis avari.
Fortunatus et ille, deos qui novit agrestis,
Panaque Silvanumque senem nymphasque sorores. (2:490–94)[2]

[Blessed is he who has been able to win knowledge of the causes of things, / and has cast beneath his feet all fear and unyielding Fate, / and the howls of

hungry Acheron! / Happy, too, is he who knows the woodland gods, / Pan and old Sylvanus and the sister Nymphs!]

The first three verses must have been inspired by what his admired Lucretius wrote in the first book of *De rerum natura*. Virgil's lifelong admiration for Lucretius's scientific poem is well known. Scientific reason, "knowing the causes of things," will calm the fears of "inexorable fate," and the terrors of "hungry Acheron." But so will the pious rituals of the gods—in particular, since the *Georgics* describes a rural setting, the woodland gods. Classical historian H. Jeanmaire quotes an interesting testimony of second century Aristides Quintilian to the effect that even Bacchic ritual practices (who would have thought, of all ritual practices!) have something in common with philosophical reason "in that they purge (by *catharsis*) among uncultivated persons their anguish before the obstacles of life and fortune, thanks to the melodies, the dances, and the play . . . that they use."[3] In other words, if one is too "cultivated," too intellectual for the old rituals, philosophy will do just as well or better. In fact, long before this time, Epicurus had already made clear in his letter to his friend Pythocles, for example, that "no other end is served by the study of celestial phenomena, whether considered by themselves or in some larger context, than mental composure and a sturdy self-reliance, just as in the case of the other disciplines. . . . For we have no use now for [vain opinions] [but] to live the unperturbed life."[4] And, of course, the whole purpose of *De rerum natura*, where Michel Serres has seen the "birth of physics,"[5] is quite explicitly to alleviate the fate of men suffering under the crashing weight of "religion." Lucretius understood perfectly the lessons of his revered predecessor, Epicurus. Here is the translation in the Loeb Classical Library:[6]

> When man's life lay for all to see foully grovelling upon the ground, crushed beneath the weight of Superstition . . . a man of Greece [i.e., Epicurus] was the first that dared to uplift mortal eyes against her . . . first of all men to shatter the confining bars of nature's gates. (1:62–71)

One must fight the terrors of religion with the rational knowledge of the "nature," the nascence, the origin, of things. And just in case his scientific effort is accused of impiety—he tells his friend Memmius, to whom the work is addressed—he defends himself by pointing out that, on the contrary, more often it is

> that very Superstition which has brought forth criminal and impious deeds: as when at Aulis the altar of our Lady of the Crossways [*Triviai virginis aram*, i.e., the altar of Artemis, the goddess who demanded the sacrifice] was foully defiled by the blood of Iphianassa [Iphigenia], shed by chosen leaders of the Danai, chieftains of the host. (1:83–86)

Did reason succeed in keeping the peace and calming the terrors of "hungry Acheron"? We may have an indication of what Lucretius ultimately thought about such a possibility in the way he ended his poem. In the last part of the poem he explains "the reason of diseases . . . and from what place the violence of disease [*morbida vis*] can suddenly gather together, and blow together a storm of deadly destruction for mankind and for flocks and herds" (6:1090–93). And he gives us a terrifying example of what disease can do, in his description of the Athenian plague of 430 B.C. Nobody knew how to stop the scourge; what seemed to work in some cases, in others made things worse. Law and order, and all the traditional sacred rituals broke down or were simply ignored. Social chaos reigned supreme. But I would like to draw attention to the very last image:

> The whole nation was in trepidation and dismay, and each man in his sorrow buried his own dead as time and circumstances allowed. Sudden need also and poverty persuaded to many dreadful expedients; for they would lay their own kindred amidst loud lamentation upon piles of wood not their own, and would set light to the fire, often brawling with much shedding of blood rather than abandon the bodies. (6:1280–86)

That is how Lucretius's poem ends. It is a depressing ending for a work designed to counteract the fear of the unknown. In the end, scientific reason is powerless against the "overwhelming scourge" of the plague. It cannot prevent the panic. But what kind of panic drove those people to such a "dreadful expedient," and to fight among themselves "with much shedding of blood rather than abandon the bodies"? Needless to say, the physical pollution was terrible, the stench unbearable. All the birds disappeared from the sky. If a dog took a bite from any of the unattended bodies lying around, it would die right away. But there was another kind of pollution just as unbearable: the old sacred pollution of the unburied human body, to which we have alluded already. There is no obligation more sacred than the obligation to bury your own dead. An unburied body pollutes the entire community, as the Sibyl tells Aeneas in regard to the unburied body of Misenus (6:150). To the people driven to such a dreadful and bloody "expedient" there was just one pollution, one source of panic, which was both physical and sacred, because when everything breaks down, these two sides feed into each other, refer to each other, endlessly. And that, it seems to me, is what is reflected in the poem itself. When a science driven by the urgent and anxious need to counteract the terrors of the sacred breaks down, inevitably the terrors of the sacred reappear, as does the need for the old rituals, since the ultimate function of those was also to counteract the terrors of the sacred (*fortunatus et ille, deos qui novit agrestis*). Perhaps it bears repeating: the fundamental purpose of the victimage mechanism, and of the countless rituals springing from it, is to keep the sacred at bay. The sacred is supposed to protect you from the sacred. As we have already said, the victim offered to the god is godlike, an embodiment of the god. The god must be expelled in order for the god to become a protector, a savior. Therefore, a science whose ultimate purpose is to keep the sacred as far removed from humanity as possible (like the gods of Epicurus and Lucretius in their distant and blissful unconcern about human affairs) is still within the purview of the old sacred.

This is why the testimony of Virgil is especially relevant here. He probably appreciated what Lucretius was trying to do better than anybody else. In the words of a classical scholar, "Virgil's reading of [*De rerum natura*] was probably the most important thing in his life as a poet (to call that reading an event would be misleading since it is clear that the reading was habitual and unending)."[7] But it is also quite clear that nobody in the pagan world understood better than Virgil the function and centrality of the sacred in the genesis of human civilization. As I have tried to demonstrate in *The Sacred Game*, the entire development of Virgil's magnum opus, and great epic poem of Imperial Rome, *The Aeneid*, is conceived and structured along clear sacrificial lines from beginning to end. The very last line of the poem (an end so unexpected that because of it, classical scholars have occasionally argued that the poem was left unfinished) is indeed the last cry of the dying victim, as "his life with a moan indignant escapes to the shades below": *vitaque cum gemitu fugit indignata sub umbras.*[8] And yet, at the same time, Virgil also knew that the choice of the victim was totally arbitrary, "an accident." This is demonstrated, in my opinion, beyond a doubt by the apparently contradictory manner in which the death of Palinurus, the helmsman of the Trojan fleet, is presented at the very center of the poem.

We should pay some attention to that apparent contradiction. Towards the end of book 5, Venus is pleading with Neptune to allow safe passage for the Trojans to Italy. Neptune agrees: they will all arrive safely except one, "one head will be given up for the sake of many" (*unum pro multis dabitur caput*, 5:815). Almost immediately we see Sleep come down from heaven in the form of an old man who, after sprinkling Palinurus with "a bough dripping with Lethe's dew and steeped in the drowsy might of Stix," pushed him overboard. There can be no doubt, therefore, that Palinurus is the one announced by Neptune, who must be sacrificed for the benefit of all the others. But then, shortly thereafter, in book 6, when Aeneas encounters the ghost of dead Palinurus in Hades and asks him, "What god, Palinurus, tore you from us and plunged you underwater in the open sea?" (6:341–42), this is the surprising answer of the helmsman: "Leader, son of Anchises, it was not a god that plunged me into the sea. For it was by accident that the helm was broken most violently, to which I was holding" (6:348–49). Furthermore, Palinurus is not only certain that it was an accident but, at the same time, he assures Aeneas that that does not mean the gods have failed him: "Neither did Phoebus fail you, nor did a god throw me into the sea" (6:347–48). He could not be any more explicit. But how can these two versions of Palinurus's death be reconciled?

I think that the key to this apparent contradiction may lie in the fact that Virgil was combining his profound understanding of the religious tradition with his equally profound understanding of the scientific explanation of the nature of things that he found in Lucretius. The sacrificial victim is at the origin of everything that human society has ever created, just as the atom is at the origin of everything in nature.[9] But the atoms, says Lucretius, would create nothing if left entirely to themselves. They would just fall endlessly in parallel, in perfect equilibrium, through the void—a situation of maximum entropy, in which energy is endlessly wasted. An infinitesimally small disturbance, *nec plus quam minimum*, a "swerve" from equilibrium, a deviation from the straight line, must occur so that atoms may collide with one another and create something. Unless one atom differs from the others, deviates from perfect equilibrium, that is, from the common downward movement of all the rest, nothing would ever be created (*nil umquam natura creasset*, 2:224). And this original difference or exception occurs in a totally accidental, unpredictable way, *incerto tempore incertisque locis*. Therefore, whether we are dealing with the nature of the sacred or the nature of things in general, everything goes back to that one which must originally deviate from all the rest. It is the one principle that governs everything. We must also understand that in human society, perfect equilibrium, maximum entropy, means total, endless violence, where the contending parties move in perfect symmetry, mirroring each other, driven by "useless fury" (*iram inanem*, Virgil, 10:758) and everything disintegrates "through the void" (*per inane*, Lucretius, 2:217)[10] unless, once again, one is made to differ from all the rest.

The accidental death of Palinurus, therefore, represents the very condition *sine qua non* for the existence of the sacred. This accident is *the* accident that must occur, the accident established by "inexorable fate" from the beginning. His head is definitely "the one that must be given up for the sake of many," as Neptune told Venus. Therefore, it can also be said that the gods have not forgotten Aeneas, as the ghost of Palinurus assures his former commander.

Of course, in the context of Virgil's masterful poem, where everything occurs for a reason, the "accidental" death of Palinurus is not accidental at all. But what does the view of Roman civilization—indeed of humanity at large—as something purely accidental, entirely in the hands of a very violent, blind, "inexorable fate," reveal about the man Virgil and what he thought about his own masterpiece? One of the best lines I have seen on Virgil is in a poem by Alfred Lord Tennyson, "To Virgil": "Thou majestic in thy sadness at the doubtful doom of human kind." It captures quite well the spirit of *The Aeneid*, which is a profoundly sad poem. Is it any surprise that Virgil wanted it destroyed after his death? He had seen what truly lay underneath the glory of the emerging Roman Empire. Let us remember that when Aeneas comes out of Hades, where the soul of his father has just revealed to him the future glory of Rome (Virgil's actual contemporary Rome), he exits through the shining ivory door, "through which the spirits send false dreams to the upper world" (6:896), not through the one made of horn, "which gives easy outlet to true shades." *Veris umbris*: shadowy things that are true, versus shining things that are false.

Pagan science knew about the arbitrary character of the founding victim, and about the violent reciprocity of the social crisis to which the sacrifice of the victim must put an end. But that did not change anything about the unavoidable necessity of the victimage mechanism itself, or its relative effectiveness. Nor did the Platonic attempt to ground it in reason while silencing the poets change anything either. All that knowledge was epistemologically correct but powerless against the workings of the victimage mechanism. It is, therefore, not completely accurate to say that "[Old religion] protects man as long as its ultimate foundations are not revealed." Or that "the only barrier against human violence is based on misconception [*méconnaissance*]." What ultimate foundation was there that Virgil knew nothing about? I cannot imagine what that could be. I am convinced that Virgil knew everything he could possibly know about the workings of the sacrificial victimage mechanism. The only thing that Virgil did not know is that the violence that creates and drives the victimage mechanism is not the "ultimate foundation" of anything; he could not possibly imagine the sacred, the keystone on which human society is built, as having nothing to do with violence.

And again, if it is true that "the only barrier against human violence is based on misconception," why do we call it "misconception"? If men know that the sacrificial mechanism works, and how it works, is such a practical, technical knowledge a misconception? What is real knowledge, the one that will kill you or the one that will save you, when there is no other criterium for deciding than whether you live or die? If knowledge of the truth will destroy you, would that knowledge, or that truth, be rational? Would the lie not be rationally preferable?

But when Girard speaks of hidden foundations or *méconnaissance*, he is speaking in Christian terms. What he is actually saying is something like this: thanks to the fact that the pagan world, archaic man in general, did not know that the ultimate foundation of the victimage mechanism is *nothing but* human violence, that the expulsion of the victim has nothing to do with the *real* sacred, the victimage mechanism worked. Of course you can also state it the other way around: it was because the victimage mechanism worked that they could not possibly know what they did not know. They could not possibly know that their violent, blood-thirsty gods, their violent sacred, did not really exist, was an imaginary collective projection of their own violence. If they had known what they could not possibly know, they would have perished. Which is quite true. But in that case, they should forever be grateful to Satan for keeping Christ totally out of their purview. Since it was Christ, and only Christ, who brought such a deadly knowledge into the world.

Thus it is not that they were not brave, courageous, enough to face the truth, like the tragedian that Girard sees as stepping back from the abyss at the last moment. They could have never recognized such an abyss as the truth, in the sense of something rational. It could only appear to them as both the truth and as violently beyond reason, the end of reason. It was not a question of courage. Nobody could have maintained their sanity for long in the face of it. By the same token we should not imagine Christ as a courageous hero facing the truth that nobody else had ever had the courage to face before. Such an image of Christ could be seriously misleading. It was not a question of courage, or *virtus* in the pagan sense; it was a question of love. In Gethsemane, Christ confronted that maddening abyss to which Girard refers, a confrontation that made him sweat blood, and he stood his ground and came out triumphant because of his perfect loving obedience to the Father. Christ did not come with a mission to expose Satan's lie, or to reveal a truth that kills. He came to reveal an entirely different kind of truth, an extraordinary kind of truth, a truth that saves—or what amounts to exactly the same thing: a God who loves humanity and does not require bloody sacrifices. It was not the rational discovery of how mimetic human violence generates the victimage mechanism that stopped the mechanism from working effectively. It was rather the other way around: the victimage mechanism had to stop working, or rather, had to be exposed as arbitrary, unjust, and without any divine foundation, *before the rational discovery of its purely mimetic origin could be accepted as such, and its rationality allowed to stand.* The loving God, the nonviolent God, had to be revealed first. It was not an epistemological accomplishment, a rational, philosophical, or scientific master stroke that broke the incredible power of the victimage mechanism; it was the even more incredible power of the loving anguish and suffering of God himself. Hence the importance of the Gethsemane passages in the Synoptic Gospels, to which Girard pays little or no attention.

We could put it differently: As far as the historical possibility was concerned for the intellectual, theoretical development of the mimetic theory, no such possibility existed before Christ's passion and resurrection followed by the coming of the Holy Spirit. And, we must insist, in precisely that sequential order: passion and resurrection first, and then the Spirit of Truth. Not the other way around. The power of human reason, which is ultimately grounded in the Truth, is, in turn, grounded in the love of God.

This love and this revelation, which will deal a devastating blow to the victimage mechanism, are offered unconditionally. But if men refuse the new truth, the truth that saves, and continue to rely on the old mechanism, they are going to face a totally unprecedented problem. However, whether or not men accept the new truth, once the word of the loving God has been revealed, the contemplation of the collapse of the victimage mechanism stops being the maddening experience from which any pagan in his right mind would fly away. Even for those who may hate it, the word of the loving God is already working for their benefit. The new, the saving truth prevents the victimage mechanism from working properly the way it used to, but the destructive effects of its inefficiency, of its not working, are also greatly diminished, far less terrifying than they used to be. Which is perhaps one reason why most men are in no hurry to come to the saving truth or to thank God for it. They really have no idea where they would be without it. Virgil knew, which is probably the reason why early and medieval Christianity saw in Virgil some sort of pre-Christian Christian prophet.

Girard really knows all this as well as I do. I have no doubt about that. However, in his single-minded determination to defend the rational, the scientific, character of his theory, at times he tends to forget something extremely important: the Christian truth in its very essence is not an act of cognition, *it is a person*, or even more specifically, Reason, the Word, the Logos *made flesh*. It is only because the truth is a person, the Word incarnate, that it is also Love. If it were not because *the truth is Love*, the truth would annihilate mankind. Without this love, the truth would destroy the victimage mechanism and leave men utterly defenseless against their own violence. But, because it is the Loving God who reveals the truth, men see the truth without going mad, explore the truth rationally, scientifically, with unprecedented confidence, without fear, giving the words of the Psalmist, quoted above, also an unprecedented relevance: "The earth, O Lord, is full of your steadfast love; teach me your statutes" (Psalm 119:18).

That is the fundamental difference between the old and the new science.

It is not the same to study the causes of things out of fear as to study them because there is really nothing to fear; because no matter how bad the things out there may turn out to be, or how inadequate our rational knowledge may prove to be, there is still nothing to fear in the knowledge of the truth. The new humanity has come to know that the truth as such is not only *not dangerous*, but will actually make for a better, a higher, humanity. Human reason and ultimate truth, the ground of all particular truths, are now in accordance with each other; and it is no longer the case that reason is at best a relatively safer, or a more effective way to handle a truth that had always been approached with all kinds of safety precautions, and which continues to rumble, as it were, in the background.

Obviously this historical transformation did not happen overnight. Once the seed of the loving truth was planted, it took time to germinate and to grow. It is still germinating and growing. I believe that its most spectacular advance was the issuing forth of the Modern Era, the cultural transformation that occurred in the Christian world and nowhere else, fundamentally during the sixteenth and seventeenth centuries, to which we are still the heirs. This birth of the Modern Era, however, is heralded in the fifteenth century by the rapid expansion throughout Europe of the new spirituality of the *devotio moderna* and its most representative work, the *Imitatio Christi*, attributed to Thomas à Kempis (1380–1471).[11] In it we read the following:

> *If you were good and pure inwardly in your soul, you would be able to see and understand all things without impediment and understand them aright.*
> *A pure heart penetrates both Heaven and Hell.*
> *As a man is inwardly in his heart, so he judges outwardly.*
> *If there is true joy in the world, surely a man of a pure heart possesses it.*
> *And if there is any tribulation and anguish, an evil conscience knows it best.*[12]

Let me quote what I wrote about this passage years ago in *The Sacred Game*:

> This attitude is the opposite of the Epicurean-Lucretian formula, or the Gnostic one. That formula said that if you know the rational causes of things in the world, you will calm the fears and anxieties of your soul. Knowledge was the way to achieve inward peace. Now instead, inward peace, for which the individual alone is responsible, becomes the way to

> a clear and unobstructed view of the world. The fears and the anxieties do not assault the mind from a world resounding with the noises of Acheron. They are the fears and the anxieties of an impure heart; the world has nothing to do with that. To a mind at peace with itself corresponds a world liberated from its sacrificial attachments. (251)

What this also means is that the loving truth revealed by Christ, the Logos made flesh, calls for an inward preparation, an inward acceptance of the truth by the human mind and heart in order for the truth to be properly, adequately perceived. Otherwise—that is to say, without such a receptive attitude—the loving truth will still be there, offering its unprecedented benefits, but those benefits will be misappropriated, misinterpreted. Men will think, for example, that the world is theirs, and only theirs, to do with and manipulate as they please, without limits, since there is nothing to fear. This perception may be all the more irresistible and convincing unless inwardly counterbalanced by great humility, because, in fact, a world from which the old fears have vanished is truly tied intimately to the experience of a new sense of individual freedom. Man's externally unhindered dominion over the liberated world out there inevitably appears to him as the expression and the ultimate proof of his individual freedom. He takes as axiomatic, self-evident, that these two things go inextricably together: an unbounded world and individual freedom. Objective, scientific certainty becomes such only when posited by a free individual equally certain of, and secure in, his freedom. This existential condition of the new scientific certainty did not obtain in the historical context of the old science. The temptation to forget that it is all a gift from the loving God is, therefore, practically unavoidable.

I find a parenthetical remark by Heidegger in his essay on "Modern Science, Metaphysics, and Mathematics" of special significance here, given the fact that nobody, I think, could suspect Heidegger of intentionally harboring a Christian bias. It reads as follows, in parenthesis: "The essential historical-metaphysical basis for the priority of *certainty*, which first made the acceptance and metaphysical development of the mathematical possible—Christianity and the *certainty of salvation*, the security of the individual as such—will not be considered here."[13] I do not know if he ever developed this "essential" link between the Christian "certainty of salvation, the security of the individual as such" and the modern development of the mathematical.

But just the fact that he could perceive such a link is in itself remarkable. Because I do not think he ever showed any awareness of the opposite, the profound link between the old science of the Greeks and "the howls of hungry Acheron." In his extensive and constant reference to Greek thinking and classical thought in general, I have never seen any awareness of the victimage mechanism, not even in his treatment of what would become a Girardian favorite: Heraclitus's famous fragment regarding "Polemos," that is, violence, struggle, as "the father of everything."

This existential forgetfulness, in my opinion, becomes clearly visible with the Enlightenment. It is not there yet in Descartes, the first truly modern thinker. His *Discourse on the Method* still carries echoes from the *Imitatio Christi*:

> [Even] the principle which I have already taken as a rule, viz., which all the things which we clearly and distinctly conceive are true, is certain only because God is or exists and because he is a Perfect Being, and because all that we possess is derived from him: whence it follows that our ideas or notions, which to the extent of their clearness and distinctness are real, and proceed from God, must to that extent be true. Accordingly, whereas we not infrequently have ideas or notions in which some falsity is contained, this can only be the case with such as are to some extent confused and obscure, and in this proceed from nothing (participate of negation) [*en cela elles participent du néant*], that is, *exist in us thus confused because we are not wholly perfect.* And it is evident that it is not less repugnant that falsity and imperfection, in so far as it is imperfection, should proceed from God, than the truth or perfection should proceed from nothing. *But if we did not know that all which we possess of real and true proceeds from a Perfect and Infinite Being, however clear and distinct our ideas might be, we should have no ground on that account for the assurance they possessed the perfection of being true.*[14]

Of course, if instead of this Perfect and Infinite Being, who is "sovereignly good and the fountain of truth," we were in the power of "some malignant demon . . . at once exceedingly potent and deceitful" (*Discourse*, 27), then even "the things which we clearly and distinctly conceive" could not be trusted to be true. In other words, there are certain axiomatic and self-evident principles (for example, I cannot doubt of my existence as something that thinks, when I do think), the truth of which I can fully trust because "there is a God who is the author of all that is in the world, and who, being the source of all truth, cannot have created our understanding of such a nature as to be deceived in the judgments it forms of the things of which it possesses a very clear and distinct perception" (115).

But we must remember now that the famous Cartesian demon, "exceedingly potent and deceitful," is far less fanciful than it may appear. We have seen those deceitful deities all over in Homer. Without them, the character of "devious and resourceful" Odysseus would not have made much sense. In fact, apart from Yaweh, who inspired such an extraordinary faith in Abraham, there are nothing but deceitful demons all over the place in the pre-Christian world. There is certainly no "Perfect and Infinite Being" who is not only the source of all truth, but a full guarantor of the truth of our clear and distinct rational conceptions—a Perfect Being who guarantees that we will not be deceived ultimately. No such God, not even for the philosophers. This must be the reason why, even though "there have been, indeed, in all ages great minds who endeavoured to find a . . . road to wisdom" (*Discourse*, 111) through the philosophical search of "first causes and true principles, from which might be deduced the reasons of all that can be known by man [other than directly by 'divine revelation,' which 'does not conduct us by degrees, but elevates us at once to an infallible faith] . . . . I am not aware," says Descartes, "that there is any one of them up to the present who has succeeded in this enterprise" (111). Descartes is thinking in particular of Plato and Aristotle, "the first and chief whose writings we possess." He sees no significant difference between them,

> except that the former, following in the footsteps of his master, Socrates, ingenuously confessed that he had never yet been able to find anything certain, and that he was contented to write what seemed to him probable. . . . Aristotle, on the other hand, characterised by less candour . . . and with no principles beyond those of his master, completely reversed his mode of putting them, and proposed as true and certain what it is probable he himself never esteemed as such. (*Discourse*, 111)

He could have brought to mind at this point the old Platonic observation in *The Laws* to the effect that "what is serious should be treated seriously, and what is not serious should not, and that by nature god is worthy of a complete, blessed seriousness, but what is human . . . has been devised as a certain plaything of god, and that this is really the best thing about it" (803c).[15] Clearly the Platonic god is not a deceitful demon, but he is certainly not a guarantor of rational human truths either.

We might call the ancient deceitful demons servants of Satan, whom Christ defeated by exposing their lies. In other words, behind Descartes' rational certainty stands "the *certainty of salvation* and the security of the individual as such" (see above) brought about by Christ, but already anticipated by the faith of Abraham in a God who keeps his promises, the same God who instills in the biblical narrator the "passionate" concern for the truth of what he narrates, noticed by Auerbach.

But the Modern Era, or an important part of it, will soon forget this God-grounded Cartesian rational certainty, and will try to establish a rationality liberated "from the revealed certitude of the salvation of individual immortal souls" (Heidegger, "Nihilism," 4:99).[16] Whether we call it Enlightenment, Positivism, Nationalism ("the development of the power of self-reliant nations"), Communism, etc., the goal—says Heidegger—is always the same: "The securing of supreme and absolute self-development of all the capacities of mankind for absolute dominion over the entire earth (4:99). In other words, in all these typically modern developments, man wants to replace God as the ground for rational certainty. But what is the role of Christianity in the face of such developments? According to the "liberated" philosophical mind of Heidegger, even though Christianity has lost all initiative to create anything new, "to fashion [anything] for itself," it still has a role to play:

> Its historical significance no longer lies in what it is able to fashion for itself, but in the fact that since the beginning of and throughout the modern age it has continued to be that *against which* the new freedom—whether expressly or not—must be distinguished. (4:99)

In a certain sense Heidegger is right. But, because the Christian truth, as we have already indicated, is not exactly a metaphysical intuition, or even a doctrine, but a person, the word made flesh, the modernity described by the philosopher defines itself, acquires its historical identity, by moving *against Christ*. Expressed in the sacrificial language with which we are already familiar, Heidegger's modernity defines itself as modernity by expelling Christ. What Heidegger calls the modern liberation from Christianity is the oldest gesture known to fallen man: the expulsion of the sacred in order to enjoy the benefits of the sacred. Had he forgotten what he learned in school as a student of theology: "the stone which the builders rejected has become the cornerstone"? Did he think that the ancient rejection would be any different this time? The historical fact is that Christ has never ceased to be the cornerstone. And Heidegger himself is an unwitting witness to it. Whether that cornerstone becomes a stumbling block, *piedra de escándalo*, against which a man will perish, or, on the contrary, a true foundation, the foundation of the truth, is up to the ultimate God-given freedom of the individual. The rebellious modern man described quite accurately by Heidegger knows deep in his heart that there is no longer any other sacred obstacle, any other victim to expel, to kill, except Christ. Christ on the cross, therefore, becomes the unavoidable stumbling block. This rebellious modern man has no other path open to him except through Christ, and he knows it. He is convinced that nothing will ever change for him in a fundamental and decisive way, except through the expulsion of the last and only victim. Only Christ stands in his way to "the securing of supreme and absolute self-development of all the capacities of mankind for absolute dominion over the entire earth."[17] In other words, only Christ, the last and everlasting victim, the blood of the lamb crucified, stands in the way of this old satanic desire to be like God.

Christ had already given man a totally liberated world, if only he would accept it as a gift sincerely, without duplicity. But that is precisely what Heidegger's modern man rejects. He wants that liberation, but he does not want it as a gift. He resents Christ's generosity. This modern man is driven by a very profound existential resentment. It is no accident at all that Heidegger's reflections on modernity take place in the midst of his reflections on Nietzsche, the near perfect embodiment of the modern resentment against the Crucified.

Resentment is the offspring of envy, and Unamuno, who could be considered Spain's national expert on envy, knew it quite well. It was he who described Nietzsche as "that poor man mad with pride [who] was also mad with envy. The history of his relationship with Wagner proves it."[18] In fact, Nietzsche, who accused Wagner of harboring an evil will to power, ended up making the famous "will to power" the universal law governing human history.[19] "Because he could not be Christ," said Unamuno, "he blasphemed against Christ . . . full of pity for himself, he abominated all pity."[20] Nietzsche's hatred of Saint Paul is truly insane. He saw in Saint Paul a man "hot-headed, sensual, melancholy, malignant in his hatred [who was] unable to fulfill the law [because] his extravagant lust to domineer provoked him continually to transgress the law," until finally "this epileptic [i.e., Saint Paul]" found "the perfect revenge" against the law in Christ, "*the annihilator of the Law!*" Immediately, "at one stroke he becomes the happiest man; the destiny of the Jews—no, of all men—seems to him to be tied to this idea . . . he has the thought of thoughts, the key of keys, the light of lights; it is around him that all history must revolve henceforth. For he is from now on the teacher of the *annihilation of the law*. . . . This is the first Christian, the inventor of Christianity."[21] Can anybody be surprised that this "poor man" actually went mad preaching to the world the arrival of a new age, the age of the overmen?

Girard has written many brilliantly penetrating pages on Nietzsche. I find his essay on "Superman in the Underground: Strategies of Madness—Nietzsche, Wagner, and Dostoevski"[22] particularly relevant here. In it Girard includes, in his own translation, an amazing Nietzschean text:

> Make me insane, I beg you, o divine power. Insane that I may finally believe in myself. Give me delirium and convulsions, moments of lucidity and the darkness that comes suddenly. Make me shudder with terror and give me ardors that no mortal man ever experiences . . . in exchange for faith in myself! Self doubt devours me. I have killed the law and I feel for the law the horror of the living for a corpse. Unless I am above the law, I am the most reprobate among the reprobate. A new spirit possesses me; where does it come from if it does not come from you? Prove to me that I belong to you (o divine power). Insanity alone can provide the proof. (75)

I think this text should be read next to the one about Saint Paul. Nietzsche accuses the Saint, "this epileptic," of the deepest resentment against "the law," desperately, sickly searching for a way to strike back at the law, until all of a sudden the sky opens, and the great illumination occurs: he sees Christ, and he realizes that he has found the perfect revenge against the law. He has found the great "annihilator of the law." In other words, he sees Saint

Paul as a madman, somebody maddened by, consumed with, resentment, who found the perfect instrument, the perfect solution, demanded by his madness. And he just wants exactly the same thing for himself. He hates the Apostle precisely because he found "the perfect revenge." After all, who is this Crucified if not the very epitome of resentment? That's it!, thinks the madman, with his face illuminated as in a vision—that is what Christianity is all about: the religion of the resentful, of the weak, of the slaves, not the religion of the strong, the supermen, those who bow to no law but the one they give to themselves. If only this superman-to-be could silence completely the whispering voice of the truth! If he could only be mad enough not to hear it at all! But "self doubt devours him." The solution to being half-mad is to be completely mad, like Don Quixote, as seen by Nietzsche. Which is why he could never forgive Cervantes for restoring Don Quixote's sanity at the end of his life, for making Don Quixote truly see his own madness. Kaufmann, Nietzsche's English editor and translator, explains in a footnote: "Nietzsche loved Don Quixote and tended to identify himself with him. He censured Cervantes for having made his hero look ridiculous—and of Nietzsche's own fears of being no less ridiculous there can be no doubt . . . . He jots down 'one of the most harmful books is *Don Quixote.*' . . . Yes, he [i.e., Cervantes] does not even spare his hero the dreadful illumination about his own state at the end of his life."[23] Total madness is the only refuge when the truth becomes unbearable, when the truth makes you mad. The doors of Hell have been broken down, but nobody ever comes out.

But the madman, in a distorted and satanic way, knows more about religion than most of his contemporaries. Everybody thinks of Nietzsche in connection with the well-known phrase "God is dead," but, as Girard has pointed out on more than one occasion,[24] that is not exactly what Nietzsche said, and he said other things as well that are completely ignored, or explained away, by all of his commentators. Here is the so-called Parable of the Madman, that is to say, aphorism 125 of *The Gay Science*:

> Have you not heard of that madman who lit a lantern in the bright morning hours, ran to the market place, and cried incessantly: "I seek God! I seek God!"—As many of those who did not believe in God were standing around just then, he provoked much laughter. Has he got lost? asked one. Did he lose his way like a child? asked another. Or is he hiding? Is he

afraid of us? Has he gone on a voyage? Emigrated?—Thus they yelled and laughed.

The madman jumped in their midst and pierced them with his eyes. "Whither is God" he cried; "I will tell you. *We have killed him*—you and I. All of us are his murderers. But how did we do this? How did we drink up the sea? Who gave us the sponge to wipe away the entire horizon? What were we doing when we unchained this earth from its sun? Whither is it moving now? Whither are we moving? Away from all suns? Are we not plunging continually? Backward, sideward, forward, in all directions? Is there still any up or down? Are we not straying, as through an infinite nothing? Do we not feel the breath of empty space? Has it not become colder? Is not night continually closing in on us? Do we not need to light lanterns in the morning? Do we hear nothing as yet of the noise of the gravediggers who are burying God? Do we hear nothing as yet of the divine decomposition? Gods, too, decompose. God is dead. God remains dead. And we have killed him.

How shall we comfort ourselves, the murderers of all murderers? What was holiest and mightiest of all that the world has yet owned has bled to death under our knives: who will wipe this blood off us? What water is there for us to clean ourselves? What festivals of atonement, what sacred games shall we have to invent? Is not the greatness of this deed too great for us? Must we ourselves not become gods simply to appear worthy of it? There has never been a greater deed; and whoever is born after us—for the sake of this deed he will belong to a higher history than all history hitherto."

Here the madman fell silent and looked again at his listeners; and they, too, were silent and stared at him in astonishment. At last he threw his lantern on the ground, and it broke into pieces and went out. "I have come too early," he said then; "my time is not yet. This tremendous event is still on its way, still wandering; it has not yet reached the ears of men . . . . This deed is still more distant from them than most distant stars—*and yet they have done it themselves.*"

It has been related further that on the same day the madman forced his way into several churches and there struck up his *requiem aeternam deo.* Led out and called to account, he is said always to have replied nothing but: "What after all are these churches now if they are not the tombs and sepulchers of God?"[25]

It is an amazing story. It is, in the first place, a Nietzschean indictment of the ordinary atheist, the *vulgaris* variety, so to speak—the one who has no idea of what it means for God to be "dead," or who thinks, as an ironic Girard has put it, that God has just died of extreme senility, that is to say, of natural causes, of pure and simple irrelevancy. For this atheist *vulgaris*, it just happened one good day that men realized God had become totally irrelevant, or had just disappeared, for they no longer saw him anywhere; maybe "he got lost," or "went on a voyage," or "emigrated."

Everything else in this "parable" sounds very much like an inverted Girard. For the madman seems to know everything that Girard knows, but then turns this knowledge into something pagan, or anti-Christian. Needless to say, Girard has been the first to notice this with great acuity and irony.

The madman knows that gods do not just die of old age. He knows that gods are killed, like his favorite one, Dionysos, by the very people who worship them. We have already seen it: killing the victim that looks exactly like the god, who is the embodiment of the god, has always been the most sacred of sacred duties. Gods are killed and then buried—that is to say, hidden in a tomb, a temple, which not only hides the murdered god, but the murder itself. And out of the killing and the hiding of the killing the god emerges again, powerful and rejuvenated, and a new cycle begins, and so on and on in eternal recurrence (a central idea in Nietzsche). The madman also knows that in this recurrence of the killing and the resurrection, everything is at stake: the killing of the god, which is only the original scapegoat, the arbitrary victim, sacralized, saves humanity from a universal crisis, an apocalyptic catastrophe, or, to use the words of the prophet again, the "overwhelming scourge."

But something strange has happened in the world. The eternal recurrence has stopped. History no longer moves in cycles, but along a straight line into the future. And it is all the work of the Crucified. He has put a stop to the recurring Dionysian cycle. How can that be? We murdered him! But instead of becoming heroes, or gods, creatures "worthy of the deed," we have become slaves, resentful Paulinian slaves. Worse yet, we have forgotten the killing completely. Instead of heroic killers, a generation has been spawned of atheists *vulgaris*, who have no idea of who God is, or that He was killed, or why. How can these people feel so secure, how can they forget so radically? Do they "smell nothing as yet of the divine decomposition"? Where will the new world order, the new heroes, come from?

Why did the madman go "on the same day" to all those churches? Clearly to remind everybody that God had been killed; to tell everybody that a church is the tomb of a god, and therefore a witness to the killing. And he was right again, except that he neglected to mention that in these new churches the killing, the murder, of God is not hidden, not covered up, but revealed precisely as a murder, a shameful assassination, for everybody to see—nothing glorious, nothing heroic about it. This is why in the presence of the revealed murder of God all heroes disappear. But the poor madman, like Don Quixote, did not think life worth living if he could not be a hero.

"Because he could not be Christ, he blasphemed against Christ." It could not be said any more succinctly. Unamuno was right: Nietzsche hated the Christian God, the Crucified, because he wanted to be like God. And yet there was something about Nietzsche's anti-Christian resentment that Unamuno never saw clearly, because he was, like Nietzsche, a great believer in quixotic heroism who did not like Cervantes at all. Nietzsche saw the profound link between the killing of Christ and the killing of Dionysos, and in general the killing of the mythical gods all over the planet. However, he also saw the killing of Christ as something robbing the foundational power of such a universal sacred killing of its heroic glory—and he could not understand that. What happened to the heroes that were supposed to spring into life out of the sacred killing? What happened to the sacred games? The only way in which resentful, envy-ridden Nietzsche could understand that was by projecting his own resentment onto Christ: Oh, he could see through the fake humility, through the hypocrisy. The Crucified was really jealous of Dionysos, of all the glorious gods. This is why he robbed them of their glory. He did to them exactly what sneaky and cruel Cervantes would later do to the heroic madman Don Quixote—to use Don Quixote's own words, "to deprive him of the glory of his victory." This is also why Nietzsche's madman could not find any heroes in the marketplace. All he could find were ordinary, run-of-the-mill atheists, who did not even know they had killed god, and consequently had no idea what he was talking about. He could have actually accused Christ by pointing a finger at all those self-contented atheists: See, that is your work! The atheists he encountered, as he looked for the murdered god, could not have been produced except in a Christian social and historical context.

What the madman saw with his lantern "in the marketplace" was truly extraordinary. What had always been in the eyes of humanity the sacred foundation of the universe from the beginning of time had disappeared from view, and nobody had even noticed! As if nothing had happened! It was totally useless for the Nietzschean madman to tell, or to remind, the people around that they had actually murdered God. The poor madman did not know that something else had also happened: the murder itself had been forgiven! Revealed as such, as murder, and forgiven, because the murderers did not really know what they had been doing from the beginning. They did it in fear of something that did not really exist outside of themselves. The threat was ultimately in themselves. That is what the Crucified revealed to them. All those people "in the market place" knew that; they knew that the old threat was no longer a threat. They knew even though they did not know why they knew. They were no longer afraid, but they had no idea why they were no longer afraid. They had indeed murdered God, as the madman said, but they did not know anything about the "divine decomposition." They did not feel they were tumbling every which way into "infinite nothing," simply because their murder had been forgiven; it was no longer haunting them. They would have certainly believed in a god that would haunt them day and night, but they would not believe in a God that had forgiven them. It was easy and tempting to ignore that they had been forgiven.

CHAPTER 5

Fiction Desacralized and Don Quixote's Madness

Let us recapitulate once again. Christ, the Logos incarnate, liberates reason from the rigid confinement in which it had been kept by the victimage mechanism: unable to break free, or simply terrified to even look beyond its walls, as in the case of the tragedians. Christ broke the stranglehold, gave human reason unprecedented confidence in itself as it faced a world created and sustained by a God who was totally trustworthy, did not play tricks on humans, and actually loved them. Christ finished the work begun by the God of faithful and totally trusting Abraham. Furthermore, together with the liberation of human reason, and as an integral part of such a liberation, Christ also liberated the human individual—that is to say, the uniqueness and singularity of each human individual—from the power of the crowd, from the violent unanimity on which the victimage mechanism was based, which only recognized the sacred victim as unique. As we pointed out, Christ sweating blood in Gethsemane is the powerful image and expression of that liberating moment.

This is the historical undercurrent, the hidden power of the liberating truth, that eventually—mostly in the last two hundred years—rebellious modern man, typified by Nietzsche's overman, will attempt to turn on its head and to interpret as a heroic conquest of his own *against* the perceived decaying power of Christianity. Christianity itself will now be seen as the very embodiment of resentment against the heroism of the human spirit in his unstoppable march toward absolute autonomy.

Needless to say, this heroic march of the human spirit is a secular, or rather secularizing, march. Absolute autonomy is inevitably felt to be a final liberation from the shackles of religion. In the eyes of most members of this modern rebellion, the heroic march begins in earnest at the dawn of the Modern Era—that is to say, as the Middle Ages, the "dark" ages, come to an end. The modern rebels sense a certain inner logic between the Renaissance nostalgia for the pagan past and the yearning for liberation of the nascent secularity.

Such a view of the beginning of the Modern Era is badly mistaken, almost totally blind to the facts of history. But it is mistaken in a revealing way. The secularists see things that undoubtedly happened, but, as in the case of Nietzsche, they turn them upside down. We should pay attention, therefore, to some basic facts about these beginnings, which coincide with what is known as the Renaissance. Our attention will be centered on what happened in the field of "poetry" as it was understood at the time, something roughly equivalent to our concept of literary fiction.

We must begin by noticing an extraordinary paradox. On the one hand, it is clear that the prestige, the quasi-divine halo, that surrounded the classics, Homer and Virgil in particular, reached an unprecedented peak at this time. Logically such an unbounded admiration for the two incomparable masters carried with it an equally unbounded admiration for the epic—an admiration that lasted for over two hundred years. We read the following in an English translation of René Rapin's *Réflexions sur la Poétique d'Aristote* (1674): "The Epick Poem is that which is the greatest and most noble in Poesie; it is the greatest work that humane wit is capable of."[1] In the words of a prestigious historian of the epic, E. M. W. Tillyard, "Every particle of all the motives that urged the men of the Renaissance to prize and to revere and imitate classical antiquity united in asserting the value, even the sacrosanctity, of the epic in its strict classical manifestation."[2]

But here is the other side of the paradox: this boundless admiration for Homeric and Virgilian epic occurs precisely at the moment when such a thing is no longer possible. In a more general sense, the Renaissance, the unprecedented resurgence of interest in the classics, is also, paradoxically, the moment when Christian Europe broke most decisively not only with the pagan past but also with Islam, the other civilization with which it had maintained close contact throughout most of the Middle Ages. The New Era was indeed an extraordinary new beginning, the opening of a new horizon, in which European civilization broke decisively with the pagan past, and left every other civilization on the planet behind.

There were numerous attempts to create a modern Christian version of the old pagan epic—an epic poem that would have in Christian Europe the central significance that the old poems had in their respective historical environments, but to no avail. There was plenty of subject matter, "le sujet héroique que sont les guerres," as we find in a sixteenth-century treatise on poetics:[3] plenty of impressive Christian warriors, and certainly no lack of wars. But no warrior and no war had any longer the foundational significance that the violence of any old warrior or any old war could have in the hands of a skillful old poet. That subject matter, those kinds of stories were no longer *The Story*, the subjacent, the basic, story of a Christian society. It took a long time to fully understand that. It was Milton who finally understood it, after he gave up his efforts to resurrect King Arthur or any other Christian hero. It was "long choosing and beginning late." But he could finally do it with the help of his celestial muse:

> *If answerable style I can obtain*
> *Of my celestial patroness, who deigns*
> *Her nightly visitation unimplor'd,*
> *And dictates to me slumbering; or inspires*
> *Easy my unpremeditated verse:*
> *Since first this subject for heroick song*
> *Pleas'd me long choosing, and beginning late;*
> *Not sedulous by nature to indite*
> *Wars, hitherto the only argument*
> Heroick deem'd *chief mastery to dissect*
> *With long and tedious havock fabled knights*
> *In battles feign'd; the better fortitude*
> *Of patience and heroick martyrdom*
> *Unsung; or to describe races and games,*
> *Or tilting furniture, imblazon'd shields,*
> *Impresses quaint, caparisons and steeds,*

Bases and tinsel trappings, gorgeous knights
At joust and tournament; then marshall'd feast
Serv'd up in hall with sewers and seneshals;
The skill of artifice or office mean,
Not that which justly gives heroick name
To person, or to poem. Me, of these
Nor skill'd nor studious, higher argument
Remains; sufficient of itself to raise
That name, unless an age too late, or cold
Climate, or years, damp my intended wing
Depress'd; and much they may, if all be mine,
Not hers, who brings it nightly to my ear.[4]

"Fable knights in battles feigned," "gorgeous knights at jousts and tournaments," the late descendants of Achilles and Aeneas, the fascinating dream of Don Quixote.

But the problem was even bigger than Milton anticipated. He was right in thinking that the only Christian story of epic proportions and significance was the story of the Fall and Redemption, but could *the* Christian story be fitted, cast, in the old heroic mold? That has been the fundamental flaw in *Paradise Lost*. "Milton," said C. S. Lewis, "has failed to disentangle himself from the bad tradition (seen at its worst in Vida's *Christiad* and at its best in the *Gerusalemme Liberata*) of trying to make Heaven look too like Olympus."[5] Witty Voltaire would put it rather succinctly some time later: "Our saints, who make so good a figure in our churches, make a very sorry one in our Epic Poems."[6] The old heroes had no fundamental role to play in the New Era. They were rapidly becoming purely ornamental, "theatrical," in the ordinary modern sense of this word. And true Christian "heroes," exemplary Christians, did not quite fit in the old heroic roles either. They really looked embarrassingly out of place in such roles.

The best practitioners of the epic, Camoens and Tasso above all, were fully aware of the problem. Tasso begins his *Gerusalemme Liberata* by apologizing to the true "celestial muse," not the fictitious one on Mount Helicon, for spicing up his Christian narrative with fictional material; and in the case of *Os Lusiadas*, the contrast between the whole subject matter and the spirit of Christianity comes to the fore just as the Portuguese fleet is about to set sail, when we see the venerable old man on the beach telling everybody that the whole enterprise is madness, "boasting of its contempt for life, which should always be held dear, because he who gives it [i.e., Christ] was so loath to lose it":

O desprezo da vida, que devia
De ser sempre estimada, pois que já
Temeu tanto perdê-la Quem a dá.[7]

The historical reality of the Christian saints looked exactly as out of place in the role of the old heroes—now turned into beautiful ornamental fictions—as the old heroes would look if, all of a sudden, they were to land in the physical historical reality of sixteenth-century Europe: in La Mancha, for example.

They would really look foolish, would they not? Just as foolish as Don Quixote. Hence the significance of Cervantes's novel. *Don Quixote* acquires its extraordinary historical significance precisely in this context. Don Quixote the foolish hero, the madman, is the visible symbol of what was happening at the time in Christian Europe at the deepest historical level. The modern novel is born as a Christian witness to the fundamental historical irrelevance of the Homeric hero; in other words, a Christian witness to the end of the agonizing need for the old heroic refuge. The old "refuge of lies" will no longer save anybody. Fiction is no longer essential to survival, because the truth is no longer terrifying.

However, simply showing the foolishness of Don Quixote's belief in the reality and the historical importance of the old heroes would not have been enough. Turning the hero into a laughable anti-hero for everybody's amusement—a poor devil to be kicked around and ultimately sent to the margins of society (to an insane asylum, for example, as happened to the spurious Don Quixote of Avellaneda)—would not have changed anything from a truly Christian perspective. It would have been the equivalent of turning Achilles into Thersites. Because, as we suggested before, every hero is a potential antihero. Thersites is only the other side—the seamy side, so to speak—of the hero. Hero and antihero belong together. They give expression to the ultimate and irreducible ambivalence of the old sacred, and, consequently, of the sacred victim, blameworthy and divine all in one, the source of all the trouble and the savior from that same trouble.

That is not at all what Cervantes did. He is indeed implacable and consistent in showing how foolish Don Quixote's foolishness really is, but he is equally consistent in regretting that such a fine, decent, and intelligent gentleman as Don Quixote (Alonso Quijano, "el Bueno") truly is should be afflicted by such a destructive disease—a disease that not only endangers his physical well-being, but the fate of his soul as well. For there is never a question in Cervantes's mind that Don Quixote's maddening imitation of the old heroes is not compatible with the imitation of Christ. Cervantes's novel, the second part in particular, is the story of Don Quixote's gradual return home, in every sense of the word, and ultimately, on his death bed, his explicitly Christian return to sanity. The spirit of this Christian saving from madness, which breathes life into every corner of the novel, also saved the novel itself from the same irrelevance and insignificance that has condemned Avellaneda's pitiful version to the dustbin of history. This is also why *Don Quixote* was "one of the most harmful books" in the eyes of Nietzsche.

On the other hand, Cervantes's book is still fiction, not history. In fact, Cervantes tells us that one of the most ridiculous and damaging features of the heroic "books of chivalry" that he is criticizing is their pretense to be history, to present their heroes as if they were true historical characters. The justly famous Cervantine irony consists in large measure in his ironic imitation of such a pretense, by telling us that he found the "true" story of Don Quixote in an old manuscript written in Arabic! Therefore, how could a novelist like Cervantes, who really knew what he was doing, use irony in writing about Don Quixote's foolish mistaking of fiction for reality, without simultaneously turning that same irony against himself, against his own novelistic fascination for the fiction he was inventing? How could he make a fool of Don Quixote and feel proud about it, superior, as if Don Quixote's foolishness had nothing to do with him as a fiction maker—indeed, as a human being? Cervantes knew that he was by no means inmune to Don Quixote's disease. Nobody is immune to it. Don Quixote's final repentance and thanksgiving to God for his mercy is also an indication of Cervantes's own attitude with regard to the story he has written and its protagonist. He wanted to save Don Quixote, because he understood his madness perfectly. There was nothing cruel about that final scene, as Nietzsche thought. The cruelty would have been to let him die insane.

The story of Don Quixote is a humble story.[8] It is presented explicitly as such by the author in a way that goes beyond conventional rhetoric. This humility takes nothing from the pride that he also feels, as an artist, for the work he has accomplished. He thinks he has done an excellent job—which was not easy, he also tells us. The subject matter was humble, not exalted; it was a funny story, the story of a fool, and, rhetorically speaking, it had to be approached accordingly. But, as often happens in this extraordinary book, the humble style becomes so much more than style. It defines the deepest relationship of the author with his novel and its protagonist. It is this compassionate humility, this profound simplicity underlying an equally profound irony, which is never bitter, never resentful, that saves the fool from his foolishness.

In this exemplary Cervantine attitude toward his quixotic fool, there is no trace of heroic nostalgia. Don Quixote's foolishness is never presented as something excusable, something perhaps understandable; after all, who would not want to be a hero sometime? It was a little bit exaggerated, but . . . There is none of that in Cervantes's novel. Don Quixote's foolishness is ultimately evil, destructive, profoundly anti-Christian, and therefore inexcusable. Nevertheless we are all tempted by it. To one degree or another we have all committed the same sin. Therefore nobody can throw the first stone. Cervantes's fool may have started as a classic antihero, but Cervantes learned rather quickly from and through his own novel, and the more he learned, the more he distanced himself from the idea of turning his fool into a scapegoat, a sacrificial victim.

If Cervantes had not saved his fool, he would not have created the first modern novel. It is just as simple as that. He saved his novel by saving his fool. Don Quixote is something unprecedented, neither a hero nor an antihero. Cervantes broke with what was probably the oldest "poetic" distinction: that between poetry of praise and poetry of blame, as Aristotle tells us in his *Poetics* (1448b24), and Averroes confirms in his commentary on Aristotle: "Every poem and all poetry are either praise or blame."[9]

Originally Cervantes's novel was viewed largely as a "funny book," and Don Quixote more or less as a classic antihero. But soon the perception grew clearer that there was much more to it than that—that this particular fool could actually be dealt with in a serious way—and then the pendulum swung in the opposite direction: the fool became a hero. But what about Cervantes himself? He was either exalted to the heavens for creating such a magnificent and glorious specimen of a human being, or the very opposite, insulted and reviled for maliciously pulling the rug out from underneath such a magnificent hero—a hero who believed in himself, unyielding in his determination to do battle with traditional and constraining views of reality. Both views of Don Quixote, the classic antiheroic and the romantic or heroic, are bad misinterpretations.

For the last two hundred years, the overwhelmingly prevailing view in the West has been the heroic one. Today it seems that nobody with a minimum of academic or critical decorum would dare to deviate from such a view. Furthermore, as we all look now everywhere for victims to save, who would dare victimize Don Quixote the fool, the madman? The two-hundred-year-old argument in favor of the heroic view becomes supplemented today by our anxious need to be on the side of victims and against evil persecutors.

In fact, the prevailing heroic view has turned Don Quixote into a symbol of modernity itself, which is seen as a triumphant break with a past in which literature and art in general were little more than submissive servants of theology—a theocratic tyrant who prevented the human spirit from soaring unimpeded in search of eternal beauty.[10]

The truth is almost the exact opposite. It was Christian theology itself, driven by the inner logic of the Christian revelation, that gradually came to the conclusion that the traditional literary genres, inherited from the pagan past, did not really fit in with the new Christian spirit. As we get historically closer to the end of the Middle Ages, this feeling of theological uneasiness in the proximity of literary fiction in general becomes increasingly pervasive. Traditional festivities in which the secular and the sacred had always mixed happily are no longer tolerated. The "war on poetry," always latent at least since Plato, acquires in the Renaissance unprecedented virulence. Cervantes himself echoes this uneasiness in the prologue to *Don Quixote*: "Mixing the human and the divine . . . is a kind of motley in which no Christian understanding should be clothed."[11] Notice that it is a Christian understanding that demands the separation.[12]

The last thing Queen Theology wanted was to keep such a fiction-making servant next to her throne. As we have said, not even the epic, the undisputed highest form of "poesy," which was desperately trying to fit in with the new regime, trying very hard to carry the new banner, could make it. And if the highest could not make it, that means no other form of imitative fiction could. The banishment from the throne of theology was particularly harsh in the case of the theater, because it had been historically the form closest to the old pagan rituals. By the end of the sixteenth century, something like the Spanish *autos sacramentales* was a rare, a unique, phenomenon in Christian Europe. That kind of theater, like the famous French "mysteries," had been banished everywhere else. The campaign to banish them also in Spain was relentless, and eventually, in the eighteenth century, it prevailed, and they were banished definitively. It took a while, depending on specific historical circumstances, but the message was clear from the beginning: the old mixture of sacred and profane—the cozy relationship, so to speak, between the old mimetic forms and religion—was coming to an end at the initiative of the sacred, not the profane. As time went on, the realization became increasingly clear that the old forms were, in one way or another, old sacrificial forms, and, therefore, profoundly incompatible with the new religion.

The case of the old epic was only the tip of the iceberg. The entire historical accommodation between the pagan past and Christianity, which had worked at many different cultural levels for centuries, was being questioned radically. Mimetic fiction could only survive on the margins of social relevance. It had no place at the center. In some mitigated sense it could be said that it had been expelled, turned into some sort of outcast. That is precisely where Cervantes found it.

But then something happened; the new expulsion did not work exactly like the old one, like Plato's expulsion of the mimetic poets from the ideal republic, for example. The new one produced something new, unprecedented. As mimetic fiction was pushed away from the religious center and became largely irrelevant and, therefore, marginalized—wearing, so to speak, the signs of the outcast—all of a sudden it began to glow in a new light: the outcast was transformed into the very image of Fallen Man in need of Redemption. This transformation in no way implied a return to the center of social importance. It was only as fallen, as guilty, as deservedly marginal, that the new mimetic fiction could see the truth about itself. I think this is the invisible historical logic that can explain the apparently paradoxical intuition of many of the greatest literary geniuses of the age. This paradox is, once again, best typified by Cervantes's *Don Quixote*: the first great example of modern narrative fiction is the story of a man who became insane by reading narrative fiction. The greatest irony of this great novel is that it is an indictment of novels. Girard has noticed a similar phenomenon in Shakespeare. For example, in *Troilus and Cressida* he notices that shameless Pandarus "has a great affinity for the theater. He keeps staging plays of his own invention. . . . [But] if every Pandarus is a kind of playwright, all playwrights are panders in disguise" (*Theater of Envy*, 158).[13] This idea is confirmed by what we see in Calderón's *La vida es sueño* when the jester, *el gracioso* Clarín, addresses the spectators with the following words:

> *There is no better window on the play*
> *than the one which, without pleading*
> *with a ticket agent, a man brings with himself,*
> *for at every spectacle he peeps, in the nude,*
> *at his own shame.*[14]

The desire that brings the spectator or the reader to the fiction denudes him, reveals his own indigence, his shame, his guilt, and that is precisely what he sees on the stage or in the fictional narrative. But, if this is so, the author, the fiction maker himself, is just as indigent and just as shameful, for his authorial desire is obviously a mirror image, an imitation, of the desire that moves the naked and shameful spectator or reader—for that is precisely what the latter sees on the stage, which the author himself has put there. "All great playwrights," continues Girard, "including Molière and Racine, have more affinity for the enemies of the theater than for its pious friends" (*Theatre of Envy*, 158).

Creative literature, "poetry," will never be what the influential romantic critic Matthew Arnold believed it would be when he said, more than a century ago, such things as the following: "[The] future of poetry is immense, because in poetry, where it is worthy of its high destinies, our race, as time goes on, will ever find an ever surer and surer stay. . . . [Most] of what now passes with us for religion and philosophy will be replaced by poetry."[15] Who could still have such high, romantic hopes today?

In his own Marxist and nihilist way, Theodor Adorno is closer to the truth of art in general:

> As a result of its inevitable withdrawal from theology, from the unqualified claim to the truth of salvation, a secularization without which art would

> never have developed, art is condemned to provide the world as it exists with a consolation that—shorn of any hope of a world beyond—strengthens the spell of that from which the autonomy of art wants to free itself. The principle of autonomy is itself suspect of giving consolation. . . . [But] art can no more be reduced to the general formula of consolation than to its opposite.
>
> The concept of art is located in a historically changing constellation of elements: it refuses definition. Its essence cannot be deduced from its origin as if the first work were a foundation on which everything that followed were constructed and would collapse if shaken. . . .
>
> Artworks become artworks only by negating their origin. They are not to be called to account for the disgrace of their ancient dependency on magic . . . , as if this were art's original sin, for art retroactively annihilated that from which it emerged.[16]

There is much in this view with which I can agree. In the first place, art is not supposed to be essentially a source of consolation. It is not a substitute for religion. Secondly, art indeed emerged out of ancient magic, and at some point it could only develop by rejecting its ancient origin. Although such a rejection, in order to be authentic and logically consistent, would have to be more like a repentance. Otherwise, how does art "retroactively annihilate that from which it emerged"? Are we talking about some sort of Freudian murder of the father? Did the son hate the father? Did he just want to take over the inheritance? Will the son become any different from the father by simply killing him and taking his place? Will he not have to reject what the father did? How will he cleanse himself from the father's guilt, or from his own murder of the father?

In his *Minima moralia*, Adorno wrote the following aphorism: "Art is magic delivered from the lie of being truth."[17] He does not quite say that magic lied *about* the truth—in other words, that magic said something that was not true about the truth. He seems rather to be saying that magic lied about posing as the truth, pretending to be the truth, standing in the place of the truth (with that much I would agree). And that lie, or pretense, must have been something constraining, perhaps weighing heavily on magic's shoulders, because once it was taken off its shoulders, once magic was "delivered," liberated, it became art all of a sudden—as if by magic, so to speak.

Not that art thereby became truth. That would have changed nothing, in the eyes of Adorno. Art became art by having nothing to do with truth. It became autonomous, but without an essence, anchored nowhere and everywhere, depending on historical circumstances. "Art's substance could be its transitoriness." It seems to roam over history somewhat aimlessly. A little bit, one might say, like the old Wandering Jew, waiting for the return of Christ to finally find rest.

From his philosophical perspective, which provides him with no knowledge about the internal logic of the old sacred, Adorno cannot answer the fundamental question posed by his aphoristic "definition" of art. How did art become liberated from the lie that constituted magic as magic? Did magic know that it was lying? If it did not, how did it find out? If it did, why did it lie? In other words, the real question is not exactly how magic became liberated from its lie, but rather liberated from its *need to lie*, its desperate need to lie.

From his perspective, Adorno cannot understand that long before what he would call art, magic was already an attempt to get away from the truth, to distance oneself from the truth, to expel it, to sacrifice (to) it. Adorno thinks it was art that first expelled the truth. He thinks it is this artistic expulsion that defines modernity, secularism, etc. But the only difference between the old and the new expulsion is that now the same thing is done without fear, with the supreme confidence that there is nothing substantive, real, out there, that poses any danger (which in a certain sense, unknown to Adorno, is true). In other words, the new expulsion of "the truth" appears to the modern magician as totally free of risk, because, in fact, he is expelling nothing. He thinks he is expelling the old truth to which the old magic was chained. But the old truth is no longer. The modern magician looks like Don Quixote; he thinks he is fighting horrible giants, when in fact he is tilting against totally unthreatening windmills. The old threat has disappeared, and the modern secularist magician has no idea how or why. When Adorno talks about the truth, he is still talking about the old truth. He is still talking about magic fears. For him the truth is either what the old magician believed and was afraid of, or nothing at all. He does not believe in, or know anything about, a truth that saves, that liberates from fear. The old magician did not know about such a truth either. The question is, who knew better, or was wiser: the old fearful magician or the quixotically fearless and nihilist Adorno?

If it is magic we are talking about, who better than Don Quixote to tell us about it?

> —Mira, Sancho, por el mismo que denantes juraste te juro—dijo don Quijote—que tienes el más corto entendimiento que tiene ni tuvo escudero en el mundo. ¿Que es posible que en cuanto ha que andas conmigo no has echado de ver que todas las cosas de los caballeros andantes parecen quimeras, necedades y desatinos, y que son todas hechas al revés? Y no porque sea ello ansí, sino porque andan entre nosotros siempre una caterva de encantadores que todas nuestras cosas mudan y truecan, y las vuelven según su gusto, y según tengan la gana de favorecernos o destruirnos. (1:xxv)[18]

> ["I swear, Sancho, by the same oath that you swore by just now," said Don Quixote, "that you have the shallowest understanding that any squire has ever had in the whole world. Is it possible that in the time you have been with me you have not yet found out that all the adventures of a knight-errant appear to be illusions, follies, and dreams, and turn out to be the reverse? Not because things are really so, but because in our midst there is a host of enchanters, forever changing, disguising, and transforming our affairs as they please, according to whether they wish to favor or destroy us."][19]

A world full of "enchanters," a magic world, is indeed a world "liberated" from any kind of objective, or stable, truth. However, Don Quixote is still sensible enough to realize that such a world must appear to be "folly and nonsense," although "this is not really the case," because, as any good Christian and Catholic knew, even if he was insane, enchanters can only play with appearances, not true reality. And yet, those enchanters can really change the knight Don Quixote's deeds, "and transform them according to their pleasure." Thus whether his deeds appear heroic or ridiculous is all a matter of who the particular enchanter is, and how he feels at the moment. Nevertheless—he wants us to understand—his deeds are really, truly heroic, for the simple reason that he is really, truly a knight errant, and a knight errant is, by definition, by essence, without a doubt, a hero. A ridiculous knight errant is a contradiction in terms. There has never been such a thing. Therefore, since he is without a doubt a knight errant, he cannot possibly be ridiculous. If he looks ridiculous, that has to be the work of a malevolent enchanter changing appearances to deprive him of his glory.

The thing is so obvious to Don Quixote that he gets mad at Sancho for not understanding: "Why can't you, thickhead, understand that; don't you know that appearances are constantly manipulated by enchanters, that that is what happens all the time in books of chivalry; and don't you know that I must follow exactly what those books prescribe or describe, because I am a knight errant, just like Amadis of Gaul, 'the sun of all valiant knights,' my shining model?" (241).

Don Quixote is not mad because he believes that there is magic in the world. That is only a consequence of his real madness, at the root of which is the fact that he has been seduced, charmed, by a shining illusion embodied in the fictional character Amadís of Gaul, "the first, the unique, the prince of all." He has been seduced by a lie, an artistic lie, created precisely with the aim of charming and seducing any potential Quixote—that is, everybody.

What is the difference between this charming artistic lie and the old charming Homeric lie of which we spoke? To put it in a nutshell, the old lie was preferable to the old truth. It was an indispensable attempt to evade the violence of the old truth. That is no longer the case. The old truth has been shown to be not true at all, but a very violent lie that generated its own deceitful way against its own violence (Satan expelling Satan). The new truth is infinitely preferable to the old lie, which is still around but is no longer essential to anything, because truth ultimately, transcendentally, is not violent and does not threaten anybody.

At the root of the old magic was the fear of an immense violence, the "overwhelming scourge," or, once again in Girardian terms, the sacrificial crisis. It was Homer's fear. The old gods, heroes, giants, and monsters emerged out of that overwhelming violence and that old fear. They embodied it, and precisely because of that, they also had the power to keep it away as long as the lie held sway. Whether they were truly, historically, real was irrelevant. Let us suppose they were discovered to have been invented by ancient and wise ancestors as a magic formula to deal with a very real and serious problem involving the survival of the group. That would not have changed anything. The invented violent gods, and heroes, and monsters would be just as good, as believable, as essential, as if they were believed to be flesh and blood. Or rather, not just as good; it would actually be better if they were not flesh and blood, not empirically real, but only part of a magic formula: a fascinating, an enchanting formula that would have the power to prevent them—embodiments of the "overwhelming scourge"—from ever becoming real, that would charm them away into some sort of never-never land of pure fiction. A bard, a singer of tales, capable of creating such a fiction would be truly divine, like divine Homer. In other words, fictionalizing was a way of sacralizing, which was always a way of distancing, rendering something untouchable.

The knights errant, the giants, and the monsters that inhabit the imaginary world of Don Quixote are still the broken remnants, the relics, of the old gods and heroes created by the "overwhelming scourge." But the violent matrix, the original breeding ground, has lost its transcendence, its sacred character. The "overwhelming scourge," no matter how violently overwhelming, has been revealed as strictly manmade. Therefore, deprived now of their transcendent status, all gods, and heroes, giants, and monsters inevitably become not only manmade fictions, but powerless, useless fictions. They have lost their protective power. They could protect against the violence of the old sacred, because they were made of the same stuff. But now that the real threat is no longer sacred, the old protectors look a little pathetic, fighting against something that is not there. Don Quixote fighting against the windmills of La Mancha is their perfect graphic image. They are fictions without an ultimate purpose. The newly revealed truth has nothing to do with them; it does not support them in any way. Therefore, they are like nothing—empty shadows. Actually, they are worse than nothing, for they become an obstacle, a blind screen, impeding the revelation of the truth.

However, if Amadís of Gaul and all the fantastic creatures in such a fictional world are nothing, mere fictions, how could they have any power to seduce Don Quixote to the point where he could swear that they are as real, as flesh and blood, as he himself is? We know what gave credibility to the old heroes, and authority to the charming singer of their deeds: their sacred character. But what do we see now as the old sacred dissipates like a vanishing fog in the new sunlight? What was hiding behind the old gods, and is still trying to hide behind Amadís? Or to put it differently, what were the old gods and their offspring hiding? It seems to me the answer is clear: behind the old magic charm lay the strictly human origin of the seduction itself: human desire, or to be more precise, the formidable, fascinating power of human desire, its power to attract human desire. Desire attracts desire. As we just said, the desire that creates the fiction, and the desire that consumes the fiction voraciously, day and night, as Alonso Quijano did, is the same desire—or two symmetrical desires that mirror each other and attract each other. Whether such a desire becomes maddening is only a question of degree.

Fascinating and fascinated, two desires feeding on each other. Left to themselves they will intensify inevitably. Beyond a certain threshhold of intensity, each desiring subject will see nothing but the other, or what amounts to the same thing, will see everything through the other—not the real other in its true historical circumstance, of course, but the other exclusively as object of desire. The true other has disappeared; reality has been destroyed as it became caught in the maddening oscillation. The two desiring/desired subjects have enclosed themselves in a world of fiction. They have lost all contact with the real, with the truth.

The internal logic that drives this potentially maddening feedback, if left to itself, must become necessarily violent. We could put it in a graphic way by saying that Don Quixote was indeed lucky he never met Amadís (the human desire that created Amadís) in the flesh. If he had, brilliant Amadís would have turned inevitably from god to demon, from fascinating model to rival—ultimate rival, the only one who could ultimately challenge Don Quixote's anxious claim to be a true knight errant, precisely because he had always had the key to such a quixotic claim.

When the "overwhelming scourge" loses its sacred status, and all of its sacred progeny become fiction and nothing but fiction, everything is reduced to the spiraling feedback of human desire becoming increasingly violent. Actually this was also the beginning of the violence in Homer. Let us remember that it all began "the day on which the son of Atreus, Agamemnon king of men, and great Achilles, first fell out with one another." How else could open-ended human violence begin except through rivals vying for something as intangible as honor, or pride of place? However, old Homeric violence will immediately become sacred in the hands of the poet, thereby turning the poetic performance itself into a sacrificial offering, a way to expel the violence that is being fictionalized, poeticized. This poetic expulsion of violence will not happen in the Cervantine view of the spiraling desire that underlies Don Quixote's madness. The fictional narrative will not sacralize, and therefore will not expel, the violence. It will not save either the charming narrator or the charmed reader. On the contrary, the fictional narrative, if it knows what it is doing, will discover its own complicity with the violence, and will ultimately confront the reader with the view of an implicit but drastic alternative: either to jump willingly into hell itself, or to give up the mimetic desire that started the whole thing. The first alternative, the hellish one, is explored rather explicitly by Cervantes in those interpolated love stories that keep developing in the vicinity of Don Quixote, and in which the knight himself may participate, as I have demonstrated in detail elsewhere.[20] The second alternative is that of Don Quixote's repentance on his deathbed.

Critics have occasionally explored how contemporary medical knowledge about madness is reflected in Cervantes's text. Such explorations, in my view, only have a limited value. In *Don Quixote*, madness is functionally, operationally defined as the fictionalization of reality. Don Quixote is mad to the extent to which he has turned his life into a book of fiction. And at the root of this fictionalization, de-realization, of reality lies the desire of the other, model and rival. In other words, at the root of the fictionalization lies the very breeding ground of specifically human violence. Fiction breeds violence as much as violence breeds fiction. A world of deceiving appearances used to be a sacred refuge from terrifying, open-ended violence. But we have come full circle now. Isaiah's prophecy has been fulfilled: The Lord God has already "laid in Zion a precious cornerstone, of a sure foundation" that has made the "refuge of lies" inoperative, no refuge at all. Therefore, in the profoundly Christian eyes of Cervantes, a world of deceiving appearances is only a prologue to some primitive, violent confusion, an original chaos—a world from which Christ is completely absent, but from which all the gods and the heroes have already disappeared. Cardenio's furious madness in Sierra Morena testifies to the vision of such a violent confusion:

> *Deja el cielo, ¡oh, amistad! O no permitas*
> *que el engaño se vista tu librea,*
> *con que destruye a la intención sincera;*
> *Que si tus apariencias no le quitas,*
> *presto ha de verse el mundo en* la pelea
> *de la discorde confusión primera.* (1:xxvii)

> *[Leave heaven, friendship, or do not permit*
> *foul fraud thus openly thy robes to wear*
> *and so all honest purposes defeat.*
> *For if you leave him in your semblance fair*
> *dark chaos will once more engulf the world*
> *and all to primal anarchy be hurled.]*[21]

This also means that Cervantes sees madness, ultimate violent confusion, within a social context—a view that anticipates some recent reflections on the subject. "Emergent madness," says Henry Grivois, "is a collective event lived in solitude."[22] This psychiatrist emphasizes the intersubjective, or inter-individual, roots of madness: "The place where madness is born . . . is also the place where we all live together."[23] In the final analysis, what Cervantes sees behind the ultimate consequences of madness looks very much like the original, the spontaneous, sacrificial crisis postulated by mimetic theory, but without the possibility any longer of the old sacralized victim that would put an end to it. Therefore, the only hope for that kind of madness is the new victim, the one that puts an end to the old victimizing, "scapegoating" process—in other words, Christ. Contrary to what M. Foucault thought,[24] Cervantes does believe in the possibility of a cure for madness, because he believes in the possibility of a spiritual cure for a disease that is fundamentally of a spiritual character, a disease of the soul rather than a disease of the body. Cervantes would agree fully with Shakespeare's medical doctor, who, after observing Lady Macbeth, who has already gone out of her mind and is walking in her sleep, concludes:

> *This disease is beyond my practise: yet I have known*
> *those which have walked in their sleep who have died*
> *holily in their beds.* (5.1.54–56)

Don Quixote will also die "holily in his bed." It is a question of sin and repentance. This is also why in that same scene in *Macbeth*, the doctor will declare that "More needs she the divine than the physician." Cervantes would concur wholeheartedly. In the end, Don Quixote will also be saved "by the mercy of God."

Epilogue

At the end of these reflections on faith and fiction, I think it is appropriate to consider for a moment mimetic theory itself, without which our reflections would not have been possible.

There is a paradox at the heart of the mimetic theory. On the one hand, the theory says that there is no such thing as an immediate or direct object of desire. There is nothing out there in the world that is desirable in or by itself. Human beings only desire what other human beings desire. As far as human desire is concerned, if there is true, independent reality out there, it will forever remain beyond reach, unknown and totally irrelevant to desire. Human desire, therefore, can only be the breeding ground of an imaginary world. Fiction and human desire belong to each other. What can desire create for itself and by itself except a mere appearance of reality, of truth—in other words, a fiction?

On the other hand, mimetic theory is also fundamentally concerned with truth. It discovers not only the *mensonge romantique*, but also the *vérité romanesque*. It tells us, for example, that except in a few works of genius, those fictional creations of desire called novels lie, do not tell the truth. But how can that be? How do we know that? How can such fictional or imaginary creations be accused of not telling the truth, if they cannot possibly tell the truth? The immediate answer within mimetic theory is that human desire lies when it presents its inevitably fictional creation as the truth: when it offers a false image of itself. But that does not remove the problem. It only pushes it one step further. Unless we can find some solid ground beyond the fiction-making convergence of desires, the accusation against the novel cannot stand.

But what could be such a solid ground? Human reason, perhaps? How can we be sure that the voice of reason remains immune to, or untouched by, the promptings of desire? Even if such immunity were possible, reason itself could offer no guaranty that its view of the world was not mediated by others, just as desire is, and by the products of human reason through the ages. As we already saw, this was at the root of the problem that preoccupied Descartes, who was concerned with finding an independent confirmation of the truth of what appears to the mind as clear, rational evidence. And just as Descartes had ultimately to rely on the existence of God as a Perfect Being who does not play tricks on humans, and for whom humans are not a plaything as they are for the Platonic god, so also does mimetic theory require a reality that is both beyond the fictionalizing power of desire and yet fully desirable in itself: an object of desire whose desirable existence is not a projection of the intersubjective maneuverings of human desire, and can be, because of that, also fully rational. Yet the rationality, as well as the desirability, of such a transcendent object is rather special. It is, in fact, unique, and cannot be fully, completely comprehended by human reason, precisely because there is nothing else to compare it with—there is nothing else that is inherently desirable. Thus we are led to posit an object of desire and of reason that transcends the limits of both. In other words, God.

Mimetic theory cannot even be conceived or formulated except on the basis of a fundamental exception to its universal law—the law that says that there are no objects inherently desirable, that we never desire anything other than other people's desire. Mimetic theory stands on faith. *La vérité romanesque*, like all truth in general, ultimately stands on faith. This is why the discovery of the truth in the novel, beyond the inevitable novelistic fiction, is something akin to a religious conversion. Girard made it quite clear:

> All novelistic conclusions are conversions; it is impossible to doubt this. . . . Romantic criticism rejects what is essential; it refuses to go beyond

> metaphysical desire to the truth of the novel which shines beyond death. The hero succumbs as he achieves truth and he entrusts his creator with the heritage of his clairvoyance. (*Deceit, Desire, and the Novel*, 294–96)[1]

What I would like to point out in this brief epilogue is that such a conversion not only saves Don Quixote and the novel in general, as we have seen. It also saves mimetic theory itself.

Mimetic theory is much more radical than it may appear to be. If human desire is always, inevitably, mediated—if we never encounter the world out there meaningfully, humanly, in a direct or unmediated way—then the fundamental question can only be, who will be the mediator between us and the world out there? In principle, the choice can only be either God or the other human, the neighbor. But the neighbor cannot be a true mediator between us and the world, because my neighbor sees the world through my own eyes, just as I see it through his. If God is not there to mediate, the reality of the world itself, the world that is truly out there, vanishes, and we are left with the deeply disturbing spectacle of human desires all converging towards fewer and fewer objects, the independent reality of which is nowhere to be seen. If God does not mediate between human beings and the world, humans will eventually self-destruct. Unless, of course, they create their own transcendent mediator, their own god. Thanks to Girard, we know now how human beings have always transformed their own internal violence, via the victimage mechanism, into a terrifying divinity, which they then try to keep away from, to deceive, to divert. In the end the choice will come down to the one with which we started: either Homeric fiction or the rock-solid faith of Abraham. The problem is that the old sacrificial solution is no longer a solution. And that is not a question of faith. It is a historical fact.

Notes

Introduction

1. Erich Auerbach, *Mimesis: The Representation of Reality in Western Literature* (Princeton, NJ: Princeton University Press, 2003), 23. Further references are to this edition, appearing in parentheses directly after the quotation.

2. Such is the case, for example, among the Lugbara of northwestern Uganda. See John Middleton, "Secrecy in Lugbara Religion," *History of Religions* 12, no. 4 (May 1973): 299–316.

3. G. K. Chesterton, *The Everlasting Man* (San Francisco: Ignatius Press, 1993), 89.

4. See Martin Heidegger, *Early Greek Thinking* (New York: Harper & Row, 1975), 102–23, and "On the Essence of Truth," in *Basic Writings*, ed. David Farrell Krell (New York: Harper Collins, 2008), 115–38. This is what Heidegger says in the latter essay: "Ek-sistence, rooted in truth as freedom, is exposure to the disclosedness of beings as such . . . the ek-sistence of historical man begins at that moment when the first thinker takes a questioning stand with regard to the unconcealment of beings by asking: what are beings? . . . . Being as a whole reveals itself as *physis*, 'nature,' which here does not yet mean a particular sphere of beings but rather beings as such as a whole. . . . The primordial disclosure of being as a whole, the question concerning beings as such, and the beginning of Western history are the same" (126–27). The emphasis in Heidegger is on philosophical man. He is interested in the beginning of philosophy, which, to him, is really the beginning of Western history. Nevertheless, much of what he says can be applied, *mutatis mutandis*, to the beginning of humanity in general.

5. Thomas Aquinas, *Questiones disputatae*, trans. Robert W. Mulligan, S.J., html edition by Joseph Kenney, O.P. (Chicago: Henry Regnery Company, 1952).

6. Wolfhardt Pannenberg, *The Historicity of Nature: Essays on Science and Theology* (West Conshohocken, PA: Templeton Foundation Press, 2008), 113–14.

7. Edith Stein, *Finite and Eternal Being*, trans. Kurt F. Reinhardt (Washington, DC: ICS Publications, 2002), 297 (emphasis added).

8. *The Aeneid of Virgil*, trans. E. Fairfax Taylor (London: J.M. Dent & Co., 1906), 262 (5:815).

9. Raymund Schwager, *Banished from Eden*, trans. James Williams (Leominster, UK: Gracewing and Inigo Enterprises, 2006).

10. I am paraphrasing from memory. Actually the phrase with the word *athée* in it was suggested (surely half-jokingly) by Girard himself.

11. René Girard, *Celui par qui le scandale arrive: Entretiens avec Maria Stella Barbieri* (Paris: Desclée de Brouwer, 2001), 140–41 (my translation).

12. Hans Urs von Balthasar has seen this quite clearly from his "theo-dramatic" perspective: "Girard's synthesis is a closed system, since it wants to be purely scientific. . . . There is therefore no such thing as a 'natural' concept of God [in Girard] . . . for Girard, religion is the invention of Satan. Here the transition from the sacral to Christ takes place without man's understanding being involved at all; thus Christ exhibits no intelligibility either. The only possibility would be for Christ's unveiling of the primal mechanism to uncover some substratum of 'natural religion,' however distorted; but Girard dismisses this out of hand and so introduces an ineradicable contradiction into his system. For, by acknowledging Christ's divinity . . . he is positing a theological dimension that explodes his allegedly pure scientism"; von Balthasar, *Theo-Drama: Theological Dramatic Theory*, vol. 4, *The Action*, trans. Graham Harrison (San Francisco: Ignatius Press, 1994), 308–9).

13. René Girard, *Sacrifice*, trans. Matthew Pattillo and David Dawson (East Lansing: Michigan State University Press, 2010), 33–34.

14. Girard, *Celui par qui*, 135.

15. In the words of Hans Urs von Balthasar: "A faith for which God, though not seen face to face, is the most present, *most concrete reality* [original emphasis], whence all that is substantial in the world receives its equally certain and unquestionable rightness, obviousness, and name-ability. In the evening breeze of paradise God walks and talks with Adam: invisible, yet as tangible and all-pervasive as the wind"; von Balthasar, *The Christian and Anxiety* (San Francisco: Ignatius Press, 2000), chapter 3, location 1441 in Kindle e-book format.

16. Pannenberg, *The Historicity of Nature*, 111.

17. René Girard with Pierpaolo Antonello and João Cezar de Castro Rocha, *Evolution and Conversion* (London: Continuum, 2007), 125.

18. Gil Bailie, "Raising the Ante: Recovering an Alpha and Omega Christology," *Communio* 35, no. 1 (2008): 83.

19. One can very well understand Hans Urs von Balthasar's "impression" that, in mimetic theory, Christ is ultimately a random scapegoat. In Girard's own words: "Il a . . . l'impression que, dans la théorie mimétique, le Christ est un bouc émissaire aléatoire, alors qu'il y a une logique dans le choix de Jésus comme bouc émissaire. Le Christ a provoqué Satan en offrant aux hommes le Royaume de Dieu. En refusant ce dernier, les hommes ont donc trouvé leur bouc émissaire déjà prêt" (Girard, *Celui par qui*, 111). ["{Balthasar} also has the impression that mimetic theory regards Christ as a random scapegoat, whereas in fact Jesus was selected as a scapegoat for a very good reason. Christ provoked Satan by offering the Kingdom of God to mankind. Mankind, in rejecting this kingdom, found a ready-made scapegoat," from Malcolm DeBevoise's translation of *Celui par qui*, *The One by Whom Scandal Comes* East Lansing: Michigan State University

Press, 2014).] But I do not think that is the point. Persecutors will always find a reason to kill their scapegoat. To me, the point is that if there is no spiritual transcendence *in the beginning*, Christ cannot be the one demanded by the system *from the beginning* to reveal the truth about Satan; he cannot be the one expected by men before all ages. If, in the final analysis, the scapegoat mechanism is nothing but a biological phenomenon, how can it cry out for Christ from within itself in order to be saved from itself? If it is nothing but a biological phenomenon, its internal logic will not even see the difference between God Incarnate and any other scapegoat, because it is only capable of distinguishing between what works and what does not. I think we have here a good example of the need for faith to light the path of science so that science does not go astray.

"To find the true and essential nature of man—says Karl Barth—we have to look not to Adam the fallen man, but to Christ in whom what is fallen has been cancelled and what was original has been restored. We have to correct and interpret what we know of Adam by what we know of Christ, because Adam is only true man in so far as he reflects and points to the original reality of Christ" (*Christ and Adam: Man and Humanity in Romans 5* [Eugene, Oregon: Wipf and Stock Publishers, 2004], 47, previously published by Harper and Brothers, 1956, originally published in German in 1952). Properly understood, Girard's anthropological discovery about the origin of the sacred becomes an illuminating confirmation of Karl Barth's theological intuition. It is unfortunate, therefore, that, even after acknowledging his debt to the Christian text, Girard should continue to think that his "scientific" discovery can stand on its own, in other words, that one can go from Adam to Christ without the help of Christ. In fact, without the help of Christ Girard's anthropology cannot even get to Adam.

Chapter 1. Auerbach's *Mimesis* Revisited

1. Erich Auerbach, *Mimesis: The Representation of Reality in Western Literature* (Princeton, NJ: Princeton University Press, 2003).

2. Auerbach, of course, is not the only one to have noticed this formal superficiality of the *Odyssey* in particular. See Cedric H. Whitman, *Homer and the Heroic Tradition* (Cambridge, MA: Harvard University Press, 1963): "The *Odyssey* has a wider lens [than the *Iliad*]; it peers less deeply, but takes time to describe. Its object, like that of its hero, is often simply to see. . . . And there is very little which Odysseus will not take time to look at" (287).

3. *The Odyssey of Homer*, trans. Richmond Lattimore (New York: Harper Collins, 1967).

4. The phrase appears towards the beginning of *La Vita Nuova*, as Dante describes his first encounter with Beatrice: "E però che soprastare a le passioni e atti di tanta gioventudine pare alcuno parlare fabuloso, mi partirò da esse; e trapassando molte cose, le quali si potrebbero trarre de l'esemplo onde nascono queste, verrò a quelle parole le quali sono scritte ne la mia memoria sotto maggiori paragrafi"; *La Vita Nuova*, in *Opere di Dante Alighieri*, ed. E. Moore and Paget Toynbee (Oxford: Oxford University Press, 1963), 2.10.205. [But because it might seem fiction to some to dwell on the passions and actions of such tender years, I will leave them, and passing over many things that might be derived from the sample from which these were taken, I will come to those words that are written in my memory under more important heads.] Don Quixote, the great fiction lover, believes that he can convince other people of the actual existence of Amadís and all the other knights errant, because he is capable of describing their physical appearance in the most minute detail: "Supporting my argument with evidence so infallible that I might say I have seen Amadís of Gaul with my own eyes"; Miguel de Cervantes, *Don Quixote of La Mancha*, trans. Walter Starkie (Signet Classic, 1964), 2.1.537.

5. *Odyssey* 19:203.

6. By way of comparison one could think of ritual phallic songs, in which things were said that were considered shameful, but because they were sung in honor of Dionysos, they were accepted with reverence, as Heraclitus said: "For if it were not to Dionysus that they held solemn procession and sang the phallic hymn, they would be acting most shamefully . . . and Hades is the same as Dionysus, in whose honor they go mad and keep the Lenaean feast" (*Frag. 127*), quoted in Clement of Alexandria, *Exhortation to the Greeks* (1919; Cambridge, MA: Loeb Classical Library, Harvard University Press, 1999), 73.
7. *Odyssey* 13:291–98.
8. Heidegger was probably the first to observe that the truth of the being-out-there, its emerging into the light, is an entirely different being-out-there for animals, "ein ganz anderes Lebe-Wesen." See *Essais et conférences*, trans. André Préau (Paris: Gallimard, 1958), 332.
9. Heidegger, *Essais et conférences*, 224 (my translation).
10. See Heidegger: "En quoi cependant pourrait résider la précellence des dieux et des hommes, sinon en ceci qu'eux précisément ne peuvent jamais rester cachés dans leur rapport à la clarté? Pourquoi ne le peuvent-ils pas? Parce que leur rapport à la clarté n'est rien d'autre que la clarté elle-même, pour autant que celle-ci rassemble et retient dans l'éclaircie les dieux et les hommes"; *Essais et conférences*, 336. [In what, therefore, could the precedence of gods and men reside, except in the fact that they can never remain hidden in their relationship to the unconcealment? Why can they not? Because their relationship to the unconcealment, the light, is nothing other than the unconcealment itself, insofar as it gathers and retains gods and men in the light.]
11. Heidegger, *Being and Time*, trans. John Macquarrie and Edward Robinson (New York: Harper and Row, 1962), 230–31. Emphasis in the original.
12. Hesiod, *Theogony*, lines 26–28.
13. "O musa, tu che di caduchi allori / Non circondi la fronte in Elicona / . . . perdona / S'intesso fregi al ver, s'adorno in parte / D'altri diletti che de' tuoi, le carte." [O Muse, that do not wreathe your brow on Helicon with fading bays . . . grant me pardon if with the truth I interweave embroiderings, if partly with pleasures other than yours I ornament my pages.]; Torquato Tasso, *Jerusalem Delivered*, trans. Ralph Nash (Detroit: Wayne State University Press, 1987), 5.
14. Heidegger sees the relationship between the truth, i.e., "unconcealment," and the hiding of it or from it, "concealment," in an entirely different manner. The threat of the sacred is completely ignored in his treatment of *aletheia* in connection with Heraclitus's *Fragment 16.*
15. Philostratus, *On Heroes* (Boston: Brill, 2003), xvi.
16. Gregory Nagy, *The Best of the Achaeans: Concepts of the Hero in Archaic Greek Poetry* (Baltimore: Johns Hopkins University Press, 1979), 116. See also R. K. Hack, "Homer's Transformation of History," *Classical Journal* 35: 10, quoted in *The Best of the Achaeans*: "Homer's transformation of history is founded upon hero worship . . . the Homeric poems deliberately and on the whole successfully suppress the post-Mycenaean aspect of Greece, and magnify the glory of the heroes in a most unhistorical but most poetical manner" (10).
17. C. Whitman, *Homer and the Heroic Tradition*, 15.
18. Walter Burkert, *Greek Religion*, trans. John Raffan (Cambridge, MA: Harvard University Press, 1985), 120.
19. See Stanley Jaki, *Science and Creation* (Lanham, NY: University Press of America, 1990): "The God of the Bible . . . is a God who is ultimately predicated on that mysterious prompting which took Abraham out of the land of Ur and set him on a course in which the sole beacon was the

unflinching confidence generated in Abraham that God would not fail to accomplish His part of the Covenant" (139). Also: "For all the primitiveness of the world picture of Genesis 2, it exudes a clear atmosphere undisturbed by what turns all other ancient cosmogonies into dark and dispirited confusion: the infighting among the gods and the lurking in the background of an irreconcilable antagonism between spirit and matter, good and evil" (140). The Girardian implications of such an original "infighting among the gods" are clear enough, even though I have found no evidence that Jaki is aware of Girard's work. Finally, the following quote in this illuminating book is directly relevant to what we are saying: "It should not be surprising that this unconditional and firm trust in Yahweh produced a warm, confident, optimistic appraisal of nature which once more sets apart the realm of the Covenant from the surrounding cultures" (149).

20. Saint Paul, in Romans 4:3 and Galatians 3:6, cites Genesis 15:6 as the key reference in describing Abraham as the father of those who have faith. I owe this observation to Prof. James Williams.

21. The reference is to Joanot Martorell, author of the chivalry book *Tirant lo Blanch* (Valencia, 1490). See Bandera, *Mímesis conflictiva* (Madrid: Editorial Gredos, 1975), chap. 1.

22. Other versions offer "vain," "two-faced," or simply "hypocrite"; in other words, pretender, the original stage actor, the man with a mask.

23. See 1 Kings 18:20–22, and 2 Kings 17:41.

24. We may apply here what Girard says in *Things Hidden since the Foundation of the World* about the passages in the Gospels of Matthew and Luke that used to be called "Curses against the Scribes and Pharisees": "In the literal sense, of course, such a title is perfectly valid. But it does tend to restrict unduly the vast implications of the way in which Jesus accuses his audience of Pharisees . . . . But then this is always the case in the Gospels. Every reading that restricts itself to particulars—however legitimate it may seem on the historical level—is nonetheless a betrayal of the overall significance" (158). I think we should apply the same criterion to Isaiah's prophecy.

25. I asked Professor James Williams for his expert advice on this matter, and this is, in part, what he was kind enough to send me in a private communication, which I quote here with his permission: "I think your point about the covenant with death, violence, and lies can be made while at the same time accepting at least some of the results of critical historical scholarship. . . .

The pact with Egypt was viewed by Isaiah as a covenant with death, for two reasons: (1) From the prophetic standpoint, the monarchy should not have made alliances with any foreign power, but have faith in Yahweh. (2) Egypt's gods were particularly associated with the realm of the dead. This is, of course, related to your point about a turn to the pagan sacred, but from the prophetic point of view God is concerned with history and Israel's political involvements. Foreign alliances entail covenants that recognize other gods.

Evidence for this interpretation includes the following:

- Assyria will be the instrument of Yahweh's anger against Judah and Jerusalem (Isaiah 10:5ff.). Notice that at 10:26 this invasion is described as a "scourge," comparable to the battle with Midian in the past and the destruction of the Egyptians at the Sea of Reeds. But this time the scourge will strike Israel. Note also, by the way, that the earlier downfall of the northern kingdom of Israel (Samaria) is brought about by Assyria, whose invasion is described as a "word against Jacob" (Isaiah 9:7). The word of Yahweh is not only what the prophet utters but the event that Y' brings about.
- The "overwhelming scourge" of Isa 28:15 is clearly Assyria as the instrument of divine judgment. The Hebrew word translated "overwhelming" (*shotef*) means literally "overflowing," like the overflowing of a river in a great flood, as we find in Isaiah 28:2. The imagery is that of a catastrophic flood. The metaphor of a disastrous flood sweeping away everything in its path

might also be a play on the location of Assyria, with its namesake capital, Assyr (Ashshur) on the west bank of the Tigris river in what we know as Mesopotamia. Nineveh was located on the east bank of the Tigris.

- As we see at the beginning of Isaiah 29, the siege of Jerusalem by Assyria will be, from the prophet's point of view, God's siege against the city. The place where "feasts come around" will become like an offering to the foreign foe. Although Yahweh rose up to give Israel the victory over the Philistines under David (28:21), now he will do the "strange work" of turning against his own people.
- See also chs. 30–31 of Isaiah on the alliance with Egypt.

This prophetic interpretation of Assyria as God's instrument (and in turn Assyria would be punished for its hubris) may strike us as too tied to specific military and political events and too entangled in retributive mimetism. However, at the core of it was the faith that both stepping back from the mimetic entanglement of emulating other peoples and renouncing the common practice of looking to foreign nations to insure survival, which was also associated with acknowledgement of their gods, were the only way to bring about the peace that the Lord intended for his people and the whole world."

26. "Who can number the deities to whom the guardianship of Rome was entrusted? Indigenous and imported, both of heaven, earth, hell, seas, fountains, rivers; and, as Varro says, gods certain and uncertain, male and female: for, as among animals, so among all kinds of gods are there these distinctions. Rome, then, enjoying the protection of such a cloud of deities, might surely have been preserved from some of those great and horrible calamities, of which I can mention but a few"; St. Augustine, *The City of God*, book 3, chap. 12, line 12 (New Advent, electronic edition), no page numbers.

27. E. R. Dodds, *The Greeks and the Irrational* (Berkeley: University of California Press, 1951), 41.

28. "It is a general principle of magical medicine, in Greece and elsewhere, that only he who caused a disease knows how to cure it"; Dodds, *The Greeks and the Irrational*, 98, 100 n.

29. John Milbank, *Theology and Social Theory*, 2nd. ed. (Cambridge, MA: Blackwell Publishing, 2006), 5.

30. Ibid., 398.

31. Shakespeare, *A Midsummer-Night's Dream*, act 5, scene 1 (New York: Dover Publications), 202.

Chapter 2. The "Overwhelming Scourge" and the *Iliad*

1. See "Beyond Plato," in Cesáreo Bandera, *The Sacred Game* (University Park, PA: Penn State University Press, 1994), 43–87.

2. Bandera, *The Sacred Game*, 58–59.

3. The *Iliad*, trans. Richmond Lattimore (Chicago: University of Chicago Press, 1951).

4. These are Achilles's words to his mother, Thetis: "I wish that strife would vanish away from among gods and mortals, / and gall, which makes a man grow angry for all his great might, / that gall of anger that swarms like a smoke inside of a man's heart / and becomes a thing sweeter to him by far than the dripping of honey" (18:107–10).

5. See C. Watkins, "A propos de *mênis*," *Bulletin de la Société de Linguistique de Paris*, 72:187–209; cited by Nagy, *The Best of the Achaeans*, 73.

6. *Simone Weil Reader*, ed. Georges A. Panichas (Mt. Kisco, NY: Moyer Bell Limited, 1977), 163.

7. Nagy believes that Patroklos ceases to be the *therapon* of Achilles, when he, in the midst of battle, becomes "equal to Ares," which is a poetic way of saying that he has become sacred, and, therefore, that he is doomed: that the sacred violence of Ares, i.e., of war, is about to kill him. But that does not erase Patroklos's individual identity as *therapon* of Achilles. It simply means that the *therapon* of Achilles is about to be killed by the sacred violence of Ares. Although the last phrase is redundant, because to the old sacrificial perspective, all deadly violence is sacred anyhow.

8. Unless, of course, the god himself, for some violent reason or another, demands such an innocent victim, as in the case of Iphigenia, Agamemnon's daughter, whose sacrifice is demanded by Artemis in revenge for a previous offense against the goddess on the part of Agamemnon. Iphigenia is simply carrying her father's guilt in the eyes of the goddess. But even here, the Iphigenia legend confirms what we are saying about the intimate association of the victim with the god who demands its sacrifice: Iphigenia will be transformed into a goddess by Artemis herself, or will become the priestess of Artemis in Tauris. In *Iphigenia in Aulis*, Euripides emphasizes the innocence of Iphigenia and the indecisive and manipulative character of Agamemnon, the sacrificer, which clearly weakens the sacred character of the killing. In the eyes of Clytemnestra it is simply murder, which will start another cycle of vengeance and counter-vengeance. In Euripides the victimage mechanism is not working completely the way it is meant to work. The tragedian is getting dangerously close to the truth, but in the end, as Girard has pointed out (*Violence and the Sacred* [Baltimore: Johns Hopkins University Press, 1979], 129), he steps back from the abyss and reaffirms his belief in the sacrificial system.

9. "The Love of God and Affliction," in *Simone Weil Reader*, 458.

Chapter 3. Simone Weil: Between Homer and Christ

1. *Simon Weil Reader*, 439. This is the original French text: "Dans le domaine de la souffrance, le malheur est une chose à part, spécifique, irréductible. Il est tout autre chose que la simple souffrance. Il s'empare de l'âme et la marque, jusqu'au fond, d'une marque qui n'appartient qu'à lui, la marque de l'esclavage"; Simone Weil, *Attente de Dieu* (Paris: Éditions Fayard, 1966; édition électronique, 2004), 76.

2. In Eric O. Springsted, *Simone Weil: Readings Selected with an Introduction* (Maryknoll, NY: Orbis Books, 1998).

3. *Payingattentiontothesky.com/simone-weil-2.*

4. Simone Weil, *Attente de Dieu* (Paris: Éditions Fayard, 1966), 166.

5. "Hérodote, confirmé par beaucoup de traditions et de témoignages, voyait dans l'Égypte l'origine de la religion. . . . Une page splendide d'Ézéchiel confirme aussi Hérodote, car Tyr y est comparée au chérubin qui garde l'arbre de vie dans l'Eden, et l'Égypte à l'arbre de vie lui-même—cet arbre de vie auquel le Christ assimilait le royaume des cieux, et qui eut comme fruit le corps même du Christ suspendu à la Croix"; ibid., 162.

6. René Girard, *Things Hidden since the Foundation of the World*, trans. Stephen Bann and Michael Metteer (Stanford, CA: Stanford University Press, 1987), 158–67.

7. See also Matthew 23:29–36.

8. See N. A. Dahl, "Der Erstgeborene Satans und der Vater des Teufels," *Apophoreta*, 70–84.

9. We should also mention Girard's comment in his later work, *Celui par qui le scandale arrive*: "Si la divinité du Christ provenait d'une sacralisation violente, les témoins de sa Résurrection seraient la foule qui réclamait sa mort et non pas les rares individus qui proclament son innocence" (73).

10. Thomas Aquinas's *Catena aurea*, Christian Classics Ethereal Library, vol. 1 (London, 1842). Commentary on Matthew 26:36–38. Online edition at www.ccel.org.

Chapter 4. From Virgil to the Modern Era

1. See Cesáreo Bandera, *The Sacred Game: The Role of the Sacred in the Genesis of Modern Literary Fiction* (University Park, PA: Penn State University Press), chapters 2 and 3.
2. Virgil, *Georgics* (Cambridge, MA: Loeb Classical Library, 1974), vol. 1, book 2, 490–94.
3. Quoted in H. Jeanmaire, *Dionysos: Histoire du Culte de Bacchus* (Paris: Payot, 1952), 321 (the translation of Jeanmaire is mine).
4. Bandera, *The Sacred Game*, 96.
5. Michel Serres, *La naissance de la physique dans le texte de Lucrèce* (Paris: Minuit, 1977).
6. Lucretius, *On the Nature of Things*, trans. W. H. D. Rouse, Loeb Classical Library No. 181, rev. ed. (Cambridge, MA: Harvard University Press, [1924] 1975).
7. W. R. Johnson, *Darkness Visible: A Study of Vergil's Aeneid* (Los Angeles: University of California Press, 1967), 151.
8. *The Aeneid*, 12:952. My translation.
9. Michel Serres points out that "the word temple is indeed of the same family as atom." See *La naissance*, 164ff.
10. Notice the linguistic equivalence between the futility of endless symmetrical violence and the Lucretian void.
11. See Bandera, *The Sacred Game*, 248–52.
12. Thomas à Kempis, *The Imitation of Christ*, ed. Paul M. Bechtel (Chicago: Moody, 1980), book 2, chap. 4, sect. 2.
13. In Martin Heidegger, *Basic Writings*, rev. ed. (New York: HarperCollins, 2008), 298.
14. Rene Descartes, *Discourse on the Methods and the Meditations*, trans. John Veitch (New York: Cosimo Classics, 2008), 34.
15. *The Laws of Plato*, trans. Thomas L. Pangle (Chicago: University of Chicago Press, 1988), 193.
16. Martin Heidegger, "Nihilism," in *Nietzsche*, ed. David Farrell Krell (New York: HarperCollins, 1991), 4:99.
17. Ibid.
18. Miguel de Unamuno, *Obras completas* (Barcelona: Vergara, 1958 y ss), 8:1102ff. My translation.
19. Walter Kaufmann, *Nietzsche: Philosopher, Psychologist, Antichrist*, 4th ed. (Princeton, NJ: Princeton University Press, 1974), 197–80.
20. Miguel de Unamuno, *The Tragic Sense of Life* (Courier Dover, 1954), 50–51.
21. *The Dawn*, aphorism 68, in *The Portable Nietzsche*, trans. and ed. Walter Kaufman (New York: Viking Press, 1968), 76–79.
22. Published in *MLN* 91 (December 1976): 1161–85. Reproduced in Girard, *"To Double Business Bound"* (Baltimore: Johns Hopkins University Press, 1978), 61–83.

23. Walter Kaufmann, *Nietzsche: Philosopher, Psychologist, Antichrist*, 4th ed. (Princeton, NJ: Princeton University Press, 1974), 71, note 40.

24. In addition to the essay already mentioned, see "Nietzsche versus the Crucified," in *The Girard Reader*, ed. James G. Williams (New York: Crossroad Publishing Company, 1996), 243–61; and "The Founding Murder in the Philosophy of Nietzsche," in *Violence and Truth*, ed. P. Dumouchel (Stanford University Press, 1988), 227–46.

25. *The Portable Nietzsche*, 95–96.

Chapter 5. Fiction Desacralized and Don Quixote's Madness

1. *The Whole Critical Works of Monsieur Rapin, in Two Volumes*, vol. 2 (London: H. Bonwicke, 1706), 184. See *The Sacred Game*, 176, where I deal with the subject more extensively.

2. E. M. W. Tillyard, *The English Epic and Its Background* (London: Chatto and Windus, 1954), 2.

3. Jacques Peletier du Mans, *L'Art Poétique de Jacques Peletier du Mans (1555): Publié d'après l'édition unique avec introduction et commentaire* (Paris: Les Belles Lettres, 1930), book 2, chap. 8.

4. John Milton, *Paradise Lost* (London: Charles Tilt, 1838), 238–39 (emphasis added). See book 9, 20ff.

5. C. S. Lewis, *A Preface to Paradise Lost* (New York: Oxford University Press, 1942), 131.

6. Le Bossu and Voltaire, *Le Bossu and Voltaire on the Epic* (Gainesville, FL: Scholars' Facsimiles and Reprints, 1970), 129.

7. Luís de Camoes, *Os Lusíadas* (Lisbon: Instituto Camoes, 2000), 191, canto 4, stanza 99.

8. I deal with the subject extensively in *The Humble Story of Don Quixote* (Washington, DC: Catholic University of America Press, 2006).

9. Quoted in Alex Preminger, O. B. Hardison Jr., and Kevin Kerrane, *Classical and Medieval Literary Criticism* (New York: Frederick Ungar, 1974), 349. See also Bandera, *The Humble Story of Don Quixote*, 12ff.

10. I am freely paraphrasing a late nineteenth-century critic, J. E. Spingarn, *A History of Literary Criticism in the Renaissance*, 7th ed. (New York: Columbia University Press, 1924), 3–4.

11. Trans. Walter Starkie (New York: Signet Classics, 1964), 46–47. All *Quixote* translations will be from this edition unless otherwise indicated.

12. See Bandera, "Introduction," *The Sacred Game*, 1–11.

13. René Girard, *A Theater of Envy* (New York: Oxford University Press, 1991).

14. Pedro Calderón de la Barca, *La vida es sueño*, ed. Ciriaco Morón (Madrid: Cátedra, 1990), 127 (2.2.1171–77). My translation.

    Que no hay ventana más cierta
    que aquella que, sin rogar
    a un ministro de boletas,
    un hombre se trae consigo;
    pues para todas las fiestas,
    despojado y despejado
    se asoma a su desvergüenza.

15. Matthew Arnold, "The Study of Poetry," in *Essays: English and American*, ed. Charles W. Eliot (New York: P. F. Collier and Son, 1938), 65.

16. Theodor Adorno, *Aesthetic Theory*, trans. and ed. Robert Hullot-Kentor (London and New York: Continuum, 2002), 2–3.

17. Online Verso edition, 2005, p. 222.

18. Cervantes, *Don Quixote*, ed. Francisco Rico (Barcelona: Instituto Cervantes, 1998), 277.

19. Cervantes, *Don Quixote*, trans. Walter Starkie (New York: Signet Classics, 2001), 243.

20. See Cesáreo Bandera, *The Humble Story of Don Quixote: Reflections on the Birth of the Modern Novel* (Washington, DC: Catholic University of America Press, 2006), passim.

21. *Don Quixote*, trans. J. M. Cohen (London: Penguin Classics, 1950), 225.

22. Henri Grivois, "Adolescence, Indifferentiation, and the Onset of Psychosis," trans. William A. Johnsen, *Contagion* 6 (1999): 120.

23. Grivois, "Adolescence, Indifferentiation," 117. See also Bandera, *The Humble Story of Don Quixote*, chapter 4, "Don Quixote's Madness and Modernity."

24. Michel Foucault, *Madness and Civilization*, trans. Richard Howard (New York: Pantheon Books, 1965), 31. See an extensive treatment of this topic in Bandera, *The Humble Story of Don Quixote*, chapter 4, "Don Quixote's Madness and Modernity."

Epilogue

1. René Girard, *Deceit, Desire, and the Novel: Self and Other in Literary Structure* (Baltimore: Johns Hopkins University Press, 1976).

Index